Speaking First

Ten more practice tests for the **Cambridge B2 First**

Jane Turner

PROSPERITY EDUCATION
www.prosperityeducation.net

Registered offices: Sherlock Close, Cambridge
CB3 0HP, United Kingdom

© Prosperity Education Ltd. 2024

First published 2024

ISBN: 978-1-915654-07-6

This publication is in copyright. Subject to statutory exception
and to the provisions of relevant collective licensing agreements,
no reproduction of any part may take place without the written
permission of Prosperity Education.

'Cambridge B2 First' and 'FCE' are brands belonging to The Chancellor,
Masters and Scholars of the University of Cambridge and are not
associated with Prosperity Education or its products.

The moral rights of the author have been asserted in accordance with
the Copyright, Designs and Patents Act 1988.

For further information and resources, visit: www.prosperityeducation.net

To infinity and beyond.

Contents

Introduction	4
Test 1	7
Test 2	15
Test 3	23
Test 4	31
Test 5	39
Test 6	47
Test 7	55
Test 8	63
Test 9	71
Test 10	79
Model answers	Test 1	87
Examiner comments	Test 1	95

Download colour test picture booklets (Part 2):

www.prosperityeducation.net/downloads

Instructions:

- Go to url
- Password: TIAB
- Select the book image
- Select content to download

Introduction

Welcome to this edition of sample tests for the Cambridge B2 First Speaking examination, which has been written to replicate the Cambridge exam experience and has undergone rigorous expert and peer review.

This section of the exam is taken in pairs, or trios, of candidates, who are assessed by two examiners: the interlocutor and the assessor. The interlocutor is responsible for delivering the instructions, handling the test booklet and interacting with the candidates, while the assessor simply listens and marks each candidate's performance.

The Speaking paper is divided into four parts, all of which comprise a different task. Different degrees of participation are expected from the candidates in each of these tasks.

In **Part 1** candidates are asked questions mainly about themselves, their background and their experiences. It starts with a set of brief introductory questions (e.g. *...and your names are? Where are you from?*) and continues with one or more topic-based questions. These topics may include things like holidays and travel, leisure-time activities, friends and family, television, etc. In responding to these questions, candidates are expected to provide brief but complete answers.

Timing	2 minutes (pair) / 3 minutes (trio)
Focus	Giving personal information, expressing opinions about various topics and talking about past experiences.
Interaction	Interlocutor – Candidate

In **Part 2** each candidate is asked to talk about two out of three photographs and also to answer a question about their partner's photographs. Each candidate must compare a pair of pictures and answer two questions about those pictures in one minute. Following this, the other candidate is asked a different question related to the pictures themselves or the topic of the pictures (thirty seconds). The three photographs and the questions are different for each candidate.

Timing	4 minutes (pair) / 6 minutes (trio)
Focus	Describing, comparing, expressing opinions and speculating.
Interaction	Interlocutor – Candidate

Part 3 is the main collaborative task of the test. In this part, candidates are presented with a topic in the form of a question (e.g. *What are the advantages and disadvantages of studying in these places?*) and a few prompts linked to it (e.g. *a bedroom, a friend's house, the library,* etc.). The candidates are then expected to develop a two-minute discussion around the topic, making use of the prompts provided. When the two minutes are up, they are asked to make a decision with regard to the topic (e.g. *...decide what the best place to study is during the final exams period.*). The candidates have one more minute to complete the task.

Timing	4 minutes (pair) / 5 minutes (trio)
Focus	Discussing, exchanging ideas, agreeing and disagreeing, asking for opinions, explaining views, justifying opinions, reaching agreements, making decisions, etc.
Interaction	Interlocutor – Candidate – Candidate

In **Part 4** candidates are asked some questions that stem from the discussion topic in Part 3. These are questions that normally touch on complex issues such as education, learning, work, healthy habits, careers, new technologies, etc. The candidates are expected to develop extended answers, and may be prompted to exchange views rather than answer individually.

Timing	4 minutes (pair) / 6 minutes (trio)
Focus	Exchanging ideas, extending and explaining answers, agreeing/disagreeing and justifying opinions.
Interaction	Interlocutor – Candidate – Candidate

This book aims to provide meaningful speaking practice while following the format of the B2 First Speaking paper. **Model answers and examiner comments are provided for Test 1**, allowing both teachers and candidates to familiarise themselves with the format and level of the exam, and the type of questions and topics covered. Furthermore, and most importantly, students can learn, through repetitive practice, what to expect on the day of their Speaking test.

I hope that you will find this resource a useful study aid, and I wish you all the best in preparing for the examination.

Jane Turner
Cambridge, 2024

Jane Turner is an associate lecturer in EAP/EFL at Anglia Ruskin University, Cambridge, and an EFL materials writer for international exam boards, universities and publishers. She previously worked as a Cambridge ESOL examiner for the British Council, and holds an MA in Educational Management and Cambridge CELTA and DELTA.

Prosperity Education Ltd.
Cambridge, CB3 0HP
United Kingdom

Dear Customer,

Thank you for buying from us.

As an independent publisher, we would really appreciate it if you would leave us your honest feedback.

If you like our resources and what we do, please help us get our story out there.

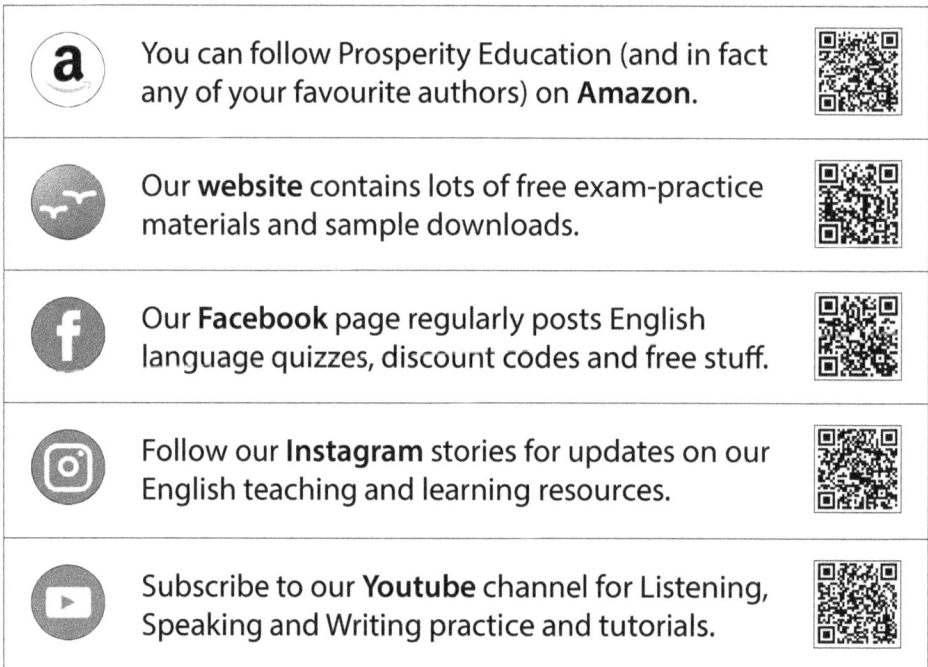

I wish you all the very best for your studies.

Tom O'Reilly, Founder of Prosperity Education

Cambridge B2 First Speaking

Test 1

Test 1 – Part 1	Cambridge B2 First: Speaking
2 minutes (3 minutes for groups of three)	

Candidates' background

Good morning/afternoon/evening. My name is …………… and this is my colleague …………… .

And your names are?

Can I have your mark sheets, please?

Thank you.

- Where are you from, *(Candidate A)*?
- And you, *(Candidate B)*?

First, we'd like to know something about you.

Select one or more questions from any of the following categories, as appropriate.

Sport

- **When was the last time you played a sport?** …… (What did you do?)
- **Do you prefer individual sports or team sports?** …… (Why?)
- **How often do you watch live sport?** …… (Would you like to watch more?) …… (Why? / Why not?)
- **Is there a sports event you would really like to go to in the future?** …… (Why? / Why not?)

Food

- **Do you prefer eating at home or in restaurants?** …… (Why?)
- **Tell us about a special meal you can remember.**
- **Have you ever taken cooking classes?** …… (Tell us about it. / Would you like to?)
- **Is there a type of food you'd like to try?** …… (Which one?) …… (Why?)

Films

- **Do you prefer watching films at home or going to the cinema?** …… (Why?)
- **What type of films do you like the most?** …… (Why?)
- **Tell us about a famous film from** (candidate's country).
- **Have you ever wanted to act or make films?** …… (Why? / Why not?)

Cambridge B2 First: Speaking	Test 1 – Part 2
	4 minutes (6 minutes for groups of three)

1 Ways of studying	2 Shopping for clothes

Interlocutor In this part of the test, I'm going to give each of you two photographs. I'd like you to talk about your photographs on your own for about a minute, and also to answer a question about your partner's photographs.

(Candidate A), it's your turn first. Here are your photographs. They show **people studying in different ways**.

*Place **Part 2** booklet, open at **Task 1**, in front of Candidate A.*

I'd like you to compare the photographs, and say **what you think the people are enjoying about studying in these ways**.

All right?

Candidate A

....

1 minute

Interlocutor Thank you.

(Candidate B), **do you often use the internet for your studies? …… (Why? / Why not?)**

Candidate B

....

Approximately 30 seconds

Interlocutor Thank you. (Can I have the booklet, please?) *Retrieve **Part 2** booklet.*

Now, *(Candidate B)*, here are your photographs. They show **people shopping for clothes in different ways**.

*Place **Part 2** booklet, open at **Task 2**, in front of Candidate B.*

I'd like you to compare the photographs, and say **why you think the people have chosen to shop for clothes in these ways**.

All right?

Candidate B

....

1 minute

Interlocutor Thank you.

(Candidate A), **do you prefer shopping for clothes with other people or alone? …… (Why?)**

Candidate A

....

Approximately 30 seconds

Interlocutor Thank you. (Can I have the booklet, please?) *Retrieve **Part 2** booklet.*

Test 1 – Part 2
Booklet 1

Cambridge B2 First: Speaking

What are the people enjoying about studying in these ways?

Cambridge B2 First: Speaking

Test 1 – Part 2
Booklet 2

Why have the people chosen to shop for clothes in these ways?

Test 1 – Part 3
4 minutes (5 minutes for groups of three)

Cambridge B2 First: Speaking

Attracting young professionals

Interlocutor Now, I'd like you to talk about something together for about two minutes *(3 minutes for groups of three)*.

I'd like you to imagine that a city is preparing an advertising campaign to attract more young professionals to live in the area. Here are some ideas they are thinking about and a question for you to discuss. First you have some time to look at the task.

*Place **Part 3** booklet, open at **Task 3**, in front of the candidates. Allow 15 seconds.*

Now, talk to each other about **why these factors would make young professionals want to live in the city.**

Candidate A

....
2 minutes (3 minutes for groups of three)

Interlocutor Thank you. Now you have about a minute to decide **which idea would be the best for the town.**

Candidate B

....
Approximately 30 seconds

Interlocutor Thank you. (Can I have the booklet, please?) *Retrieve **Part 3** booklet.*

Part 4
4 minutes (6 minutes for groups of three)

Interlocutor *Use the following questions, in order, as appropriate:*

| *Select any of the following prompts, as appropriate:* |
| • What do you think? |
| • Do you agree? |
| • And you? |

As well as young professionals, what other types of people might cities want to attract? ...... (Why?)

Some people say that it is unfair for cities to receive so much investment and that rural areas should be improved instead. **Do you agree?** ...... (Why? / Why not?)

What can companies do to help staff who have just moved to the area? ......

What are the most enjoyable things to do on a city break in (candidate's country)?

Some people say that remote working will transform cities. **What do you think?**

Would you agree that cities are designed for the needs of young people? ...... (Why? / Why not?)

Interlocutor Thank you. That is the end of the test.

Cambridge B2 First: Speaking

Test 1 – Part 3
Booklet

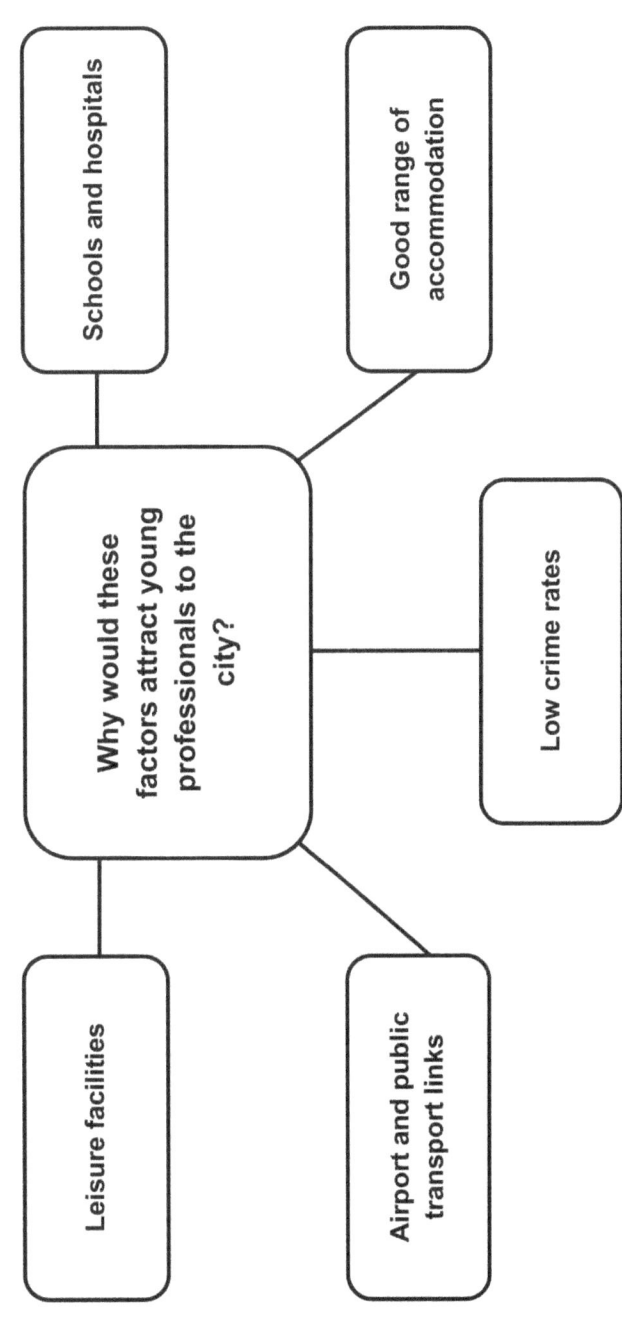

Speaking First — Mark sheet

| Date | DD | MM | YY |

Candidate _____

Marks available

Grammar and vocabulary	0	1	1.5	2	2.5	3	3.5	4	4.5	5
Discourse Management	0	1	1.5	2	2.5	3	3.5	4	4.5	5
Pronunciation	0	1	1.5	2	2.5	3	3.5	4	4.5	5
Interactive Communication	0	1	1.5	2	2.5	3	3.5	4	4.5	5

Item descriptors

Grammar and vocabulary *Control* *Range*	• Degree of control of grammatical forms. • Range of grammatical forms used.
Discourse Management *Extent* *Relevance* *Coherence* *Cohesion*	• Stretches of language produced. • Relevance of contributions and organisation of ideas. • Use of appropriate cohesive devices and discourse markers.
Pronunciation *Intonation* *Stress* *Individual sounds*	• Intelligibility • Intonation • Word stress • Individual sounds
Interactive Communication *Initiating* *Responding* *Development*	• Initiating, responding and linking contributions to other speakers' interventions. • Maintaining and developing interaction, and negotiating towards an outcome.

Cambridge B2 First Speaking

Test 2

Test 2 – Part 1
2 minutes (3 minutes for groups of three)

Cambridge B2 First: Speaking

Candidates' background

Good morning/afternoon/evening. My name is …………… and this is my colleague …………… .

And your names are?

Can I have your mark sheets, please?

Thank you.

- Where are you from, *(Candidate A)*?
- And you, *(Candidate B)*?

First, we'd like to know something about you.

Select one or more questions from any of the following categories, as appropriate.

Travel

- **Can you tell us about an interesting place you have visited?** …… **(Why was it interesting?)**
- **Would you rather travel alone or with friends?** …… **(Why?)**
- **What do you like to do when you're on holiday?** …… **(Why?)**
- **Which country or place would you like to visit in the future?** …… **(Why?)**

Music

- **Do you prefer listening to recorded music or going to live concerts?** …… **(Why?)**
- **Is there a singer or band you particularly admire?** …… **(Tell us about them.)**
- **How often do you listen to music?** …… **(Why do you listen to music?)**
- **Is there a musical instrument you'd like to learn to play?** …… **(Which one?)** …… **(Why?)**

Friendship

- **Tell us about a friend who is important to you.**
- **Is having a lot of online friends important to you?** …… **(Why? / Why not?)**
- **What are the most important qualities you expect in a friend?** …… **(Why?)**
- **What do you enjoy doing with your friends?** …… **(Why?)**

Cambridge B2 First: Speaking	Test 2 – Part 2
	4 minutes (6 minutes for groups of three)

1 Spending time with animals	2 Eating out

Interlocutor   In this part of the test, I'm going to give each of you two photographs. I'd like you to talk about your photographs on your own for about a minute, and also to answer a question about your partner's photographs.

(Candidate A), it's your turn first. Here are your photographs. They show **people spending time with animals in different ways**.

Place Part 2 booklet, open at Task 1, in front of Candidate A.

I'd like you to compare the photographs, and say **what you think the people are enjoying about spending time with these animals**.

All right?

Candidate A

1 minute

Interlocutor   Thank you.

(Candidate B), **do you find spending time with animals relaxing? …… (Why? / Why not?)**

Candidate B

Approximately 30 seconds

Interlocutor   Thank you. (Can I have the booklet, please?) *Retrieve Part 2 booklet.*

Now, *(Candidate B)*, here are your photographs. They show **people eating out in different places**.

Place Part 2 booklet, open at Task 2, in front of Candidate B.

I'd like you to compare the photographs, and say **why you think the people have chosen to eat out in these different places.**

All right?

Candidate B

1 minute

Interlocutor   Thank you.

(Candidate A), **when you're eating out, do you prefer trying new places or going to familiar places? …… (Why?)**

Candidate A

Approximately 30 seconds

Interlocutor   Thank you. (Can I have the booklet, please?) *Retrieve Part 2 booklet.*

Test 2 – Part 2 — Cambridge B2 First: Speaking
Booklet 1

What are the people enjoying about spending time with these animals?

Cambridge B2 First: Speaking

Test 2 – Part 2
Booklet 2

Why have the people chosen to eat out in these places?

Test 2 – Part 3
4 minutes (5 minutes for groups of three)

Cambridge B2 First: Speaking

Promoting sport at school

Interlocutor   Now, I'd like you to talk about something together for about two minutes *(3 minutes for groups of three)*.

I'd like you to imagine that a school wants to encourage its students to take up sport and be more active. Here are some ideas they are thinking about and a question for you to discuss. First you have some time to look at the task.

Place Part 3 booklet, open at Task 3, in front of the candidates. Allow 15 seconds.

Now, talk to each other about **why these ideas would make students want to be more active.**

Candidate A

....

2 minutes (3 minutes for groups of three)

Interlocutor   Thank you. Now you have about a minute to decide **which idea would be the best for the school.**

Candidate B

....

Approximately 30 seconds

Interlocutor   Thank you. (Can I have the booklet, please?) *Retrieve Part 3 booklet.*

Part 4
4 minutes (6 minutes for groups of three)

Interlocutor   *Use the following questions, in order, as appropriate:*

| *Select any of the following prompts, as appropriate:* |
| • What do you think? |
| • Do you agree? |
| • And you? |

What might make students reluctant to do sport? …… (Why?)

Some people say that the fitness industry cares more about profits than people's health. Do you agree? …… (Why? / Why not?)

In your opinion, why do some people want to do extreme sports? …… (Why? / Why not?)

What are the most popular sports in (candidate's country)**?**

Some people say that fitness apps and social media are transforming the way people exercise. What do you think?

Would you agree that the mental benefits of being active are more important than the physical benefits? …… (Why? / Why not?)

Interlocutor   Thank you. That is the end of the test.

Cambridge B2 First: Speaking

Test 2 – Part 3
Booklet

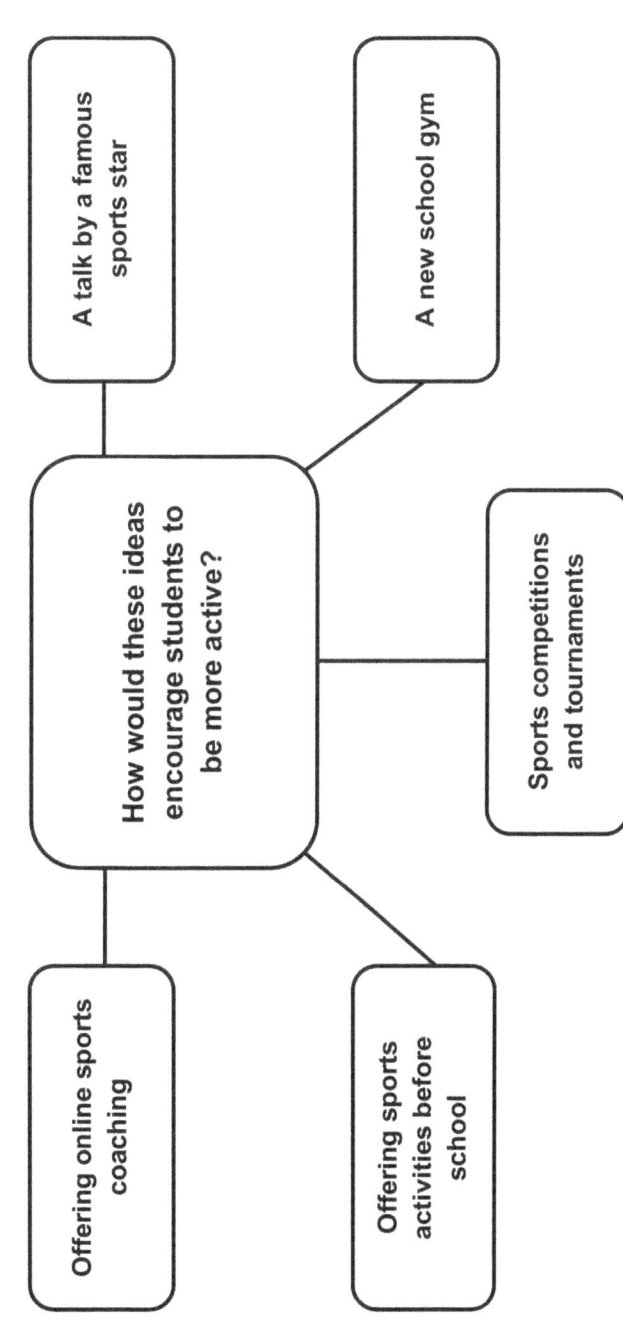

Speaking First — Mark sheet

Date | DD | MM | YY |

Candidate _____

Marks available

Grammar and vocabulary	0	1	1.5	2	2.5	3	3.5	4	4.5	5
Discourse Management	0	1	1.5	2	2.5	3	3.5	4	4.5	5
Pronunciation	0	1	1.5	2	2.5	3	3.5	4	4.5	5
Interactive Communication	0	1	1.5	2	2.5	3	3.5	4	4.5	5

Item descriptors

Grammar and vocabulary *Control* *Range*	• Degree of control of grammatical forms. • Range of grammatical forms used.
Discourse Management *Extent* *Relevance* *Coherence* *Cohesion*	• Stretches of language produced. • Relevance of contributions and organisation of ideas. • Use of appropriate cohesive devices and discourse markers.
Pronunciation *Intonation* *Stress* *Individual sounds*	• Intelligibility • Intonation • Word stress • Individual sounds
Interactive Communication *Initiating* *Responding* *Development*	• Initiating, responding and linking contributions to other speakers' interventions. • Maintaining and developing interaction, and negotiating towards an outcome.

Cambridge B2 First Speaking

Test 3

Test 3 – Part 1	Cambridge B2 First: Speaking
2 minutes (3 minutes for groups of three)	

Candidates' background

Good morning/afternoon/evening. My name is …………… and this is my colleague …………… .

And your names are?

Can I have your mark sheets, please?

Thank you.

- Where are you from, *(Candidate A)*?
- And you, *(Candidate B)*?

First, we'd like to know something about you.

Select one or more questions from any of the following categories, as appropriate.

Attitudes to work

- **What would be your dream job? …… (Why?)**
- **How important is work to you? …… (Why?)**
- **Have you ever wanted to start your business? …… (Why? / Why not?)**
- **Tell us about a professional achievement or ambition that is important to you.**

Clothes

- **How would you describe your taste in clothes? …… (Why?)**
- **Tell us about a special piece of clothing that you have owned.**
- **How important is following fashion trends to you? …… (Why?)**
- **Do you enjoy shopping for clothes? …… (Why? / Why not?)**

Technology

- **Tell us about a gadget or device that you enjoy using.**
- **Are you keen to try new technology or gadgets when they come out? …… (Why? / Why not?)**
- **What is important to you when you're choosing new technology? …… (Why?)**
- **Have you ever tried to limit your screen time? …… (Why? / Why not?)**

Cambridge B2 First: Speaking	Test 3 – Part 2
	4 minutes (6 minutes for groups of three)

1 Dealing with problems	2 Relaxation

Interlocutor In this part of the test, I'm going to give each of you two photographs. I'd like you to talk about your photographs on your own for about a minute, and also to answer a question about your partner's photographs.

(Candidate A), it's your turn first. Here are your photographs. They show **people who have just discovered a problem in different situations**.

*Place **Part 2** booklet, open at **Task 1**, in front of Candidate A.*

I'd like you to compare the photographs, and say **what you think the people might be about to do in these situations.**

All right?

Candidate A

....

1 minute

Interlocutor Thank you.

(Candidate B), **do you find it easy to solve unexpected problems? …… (Why? / Why not?)**

Candidate B

....

Approximately 30 seconds

Interlocutor Thank you. (Can I have the booklet, please?) *Retrieve **Part 2** booklet.*

Now, (Candidate B), here are your photographs. They show **people relaxing in different ways**.

*Place **Part 2** booklet, open at **Task 2**, in front of Candidate B.*

I'd like you to compare the photographs, and say **what you think the people find relaxing about these activities**.

All right?

Candidate B

....

1 minute

Interlocutor Thank you.

(Candidate A), **which of the activities would you choose if you wanted relaxation? …… (Why?)**

Candidate A

....

Approximately 30 seconds

Interlocutor Thank you. (Can I have the booklet, please?) *Retrieve **Part 2** booklet.*

Cambridge B2 First: Speaking

Test 3 – Part 2
Booklet 1

What might the people be about to do in these situations?

Cambridge B2 First: Speaking

Test 3 – Part 2
Booklet 2

What might the people find relaxing about these situations?

Test 3 – Part 3
4 minutes (5 minutes for groups of three)

Cambridge B2 First: Speaking

Saving money

Interlocutor Now, I'd like you to talk about something together for about two minutes *(3 minutes for groups of three)*.

I'd like you to imagine that a magazine is planning an article giving advice to people who want to save money. Here are some ideas they are thinking about and a question for you to discuss. First you have some time to look at the task.

*Place **Part 3** booklet, open at **Task 3**, in front of the candidates. Allow 15 seconds.*

Now, talk to each other about **how these suggestions could change people's spending habits.**

Candidate A

....

2 minutes (3 minutes for groups of three)

Interlocutor Thank you. Now you have about a minute to decide **which idea should be the main focus of the article.**

Candidate B

....

Approximately 30 seconds

Interlocutor Thank you. (Can I have the booklet, please?) *Retrieve **Part 3** booklet.*

Part 4
4 minutes (6 minutes for groups of three)

Interlocutor *Use the following questions, in order, as appropriate:*

| *Select any of the following prompts, as appropriate:* |
| • **What do you think?** |
| • **Do you agree?** |
| • **And you?** |

Do you think people are taught enough about saving money? ...... (Why? / Why not?)

Why do you think some people might dislike talking about money?

Some people say that you shouldn't borrow money from friends or agree to lend them money. What do you think? ...... (Why?)

In what ways might money affect a friendship or relationship? ...... (Why?)

Are there any advantages of paying for things in cash rather than by bank cards? ...... (Why? / Why not?)

Is having a high-paying job considered important in (candidate's country)**? ...... (Why? / Why not?)**

Interlocutor Thank you. That is the end of the test.

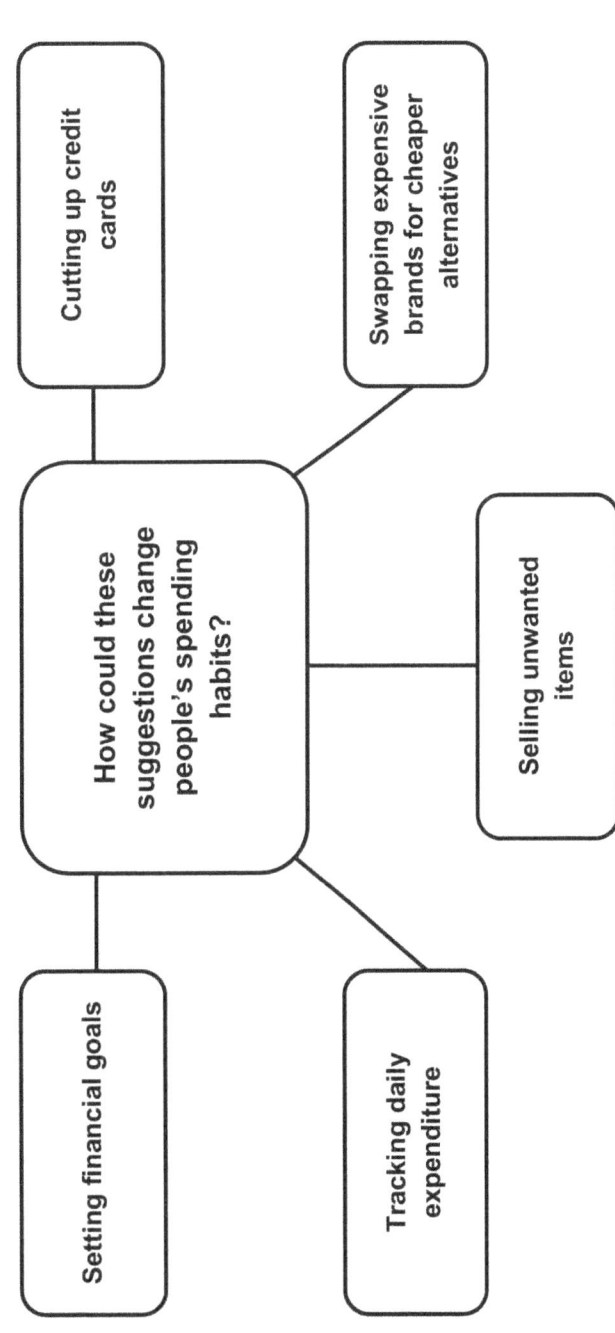

Speaking First   Mark sheet

Date | DD | MM | YY | **Candidate** _____

Marks available

Grammar and vocabulary	0	1	1.5	2	2.5	3	3.5	4	4.5	5
Discourse Management	0	1	1.5	2	2.5	3	3.5	4	4.5	5
Pronunciation	0	1	1.5	2	2.5	3	3.5	4	4.5	5
Interactive Communication	0	1	1.5	2	2.5	3	3.5	4	4.5	5

Item descriptors

Grammar and vocabulary *Control* *Range*	• Degree of control of grammatical forms. • Range of grammatical forms used.
Discourse Management *Extent* *Relevance* *Coherence* *Cohesion*	• Stretches of language produced. • Relevance of contributions and organisation of ideas. • Use of appropriate cohesive devices and discourse markers.
Pronunciation *Intonation* *Stress* *Individual sounds*	• Intelligibility • Intonation • Word stress • Individual sounds
Interactive Communication *Initiating* *Responding* *Development*	• Initiating, responding and linking contributions to other speakers' interventions. • Maintaining and developing interaction, and negotiating towards an outcome.

Cambridge B2 First Speaking

Test 4

Test 4 – Part 1
2 minutes (3 minutes for groups of three)

Cambridge B2 First: Speaking

Candidates' background

Good morning/afternoon/evening. My name is …………… and this is my colleague …………… .

And your names are?

Can I have your mark sheets, please?

Thank you.

- Where are you from, *(Candidate A)*?
- And you, *(Candidate B)*?

First, we'd like to know something about you.

Select one or more questions from any of the following categories, as appropriate.

Home town or city

- Tell us about where you grew up or live.
- What do you like most about your home town? …… (Why?)
- Is there anything that could be improved about your home town? …… (Why? / Why not?)
- What suggestions would you give to someone visiting your home town? …… (Why?)

Staying healthy

- Would you say that you lead a healthy lifestyle? …… (Why? / Why not?)
- Which aspects of health are most important to you? …… (Why?)
- What do you find most useful when trying to stay healthy? …… (Why?)
- Do you prefer being active or relaxing in your free time? …… (Why? / Why not?)

Comedy

- Tell us about a TV show that you find funny.
- Do you prefer comedy or drama? …… (Why?)
- Is live comedy popular in (candidate's country)? …… (Why? / Why not?)
- How would other people describe your sense of humour? …… (Why?)

Cambridge B2 First: Speaking	Test 4 – Part 2
	4 minutes (6 minutes for groups of three)

1 Learning about a place	2 Teaching

Interlocutor In this part of the test, I'm going to give each of you two photographs. I'd like you to talk about your photographs on your own for about a minute, and also to answer a question about your partner's photographs.

(Candidate A), it's your turn first. Here are your photographs. They show **people who are learning about a place.**

*Place **Part 2** booklet, open at **Task 1**, in front of Candidate A.*

I'd like you to compare the photographs, and say **what type of information the people might be learning in these situations.**

All right?

Candidate A

....

1 minute

Interlocutor Thank you.

(Candidate B), **how much research do you do before you visit a new place? …… (Why?)**

Candidate B

....

Approximately 30 seconds

Interlocutor Thank you. (Can I have the booklet, please?) *Retrieve **Part 2** booklet.*

Now, *(Candidate B)*, here are your photographs. They show **people teaching in different situations**.

*Place **Part 2** booklet, open at **Task 2**, in front of Candidate B.*

I'd like you to compare the photographs, and **say how important the size of the class might be in these different situations.**

All right?

Candidate B

....

1 minute

Interlocutor Thank you.

(Candidate A), **which of these situations would you prefer to be in? …… (Why?)**

Candidate A

....

Approximately 30 seconds

Interlocutor Thank you. (Can I have the booklet, please?) *Retrieve **Part 2** booklet.*

Test 4 – Part 2
Booklet 1

Cambridge B2 First: Speaking

What type of information might the people be learning?

How important might the size of the class be in these situations?

Test 4 – Part 3
4 minutes (5 minutes for groups of three)

Cambridge B2 First: Speaking

Screen time

Interlocutor Now, I'd like you to talk about something together for about two minutes *(3 minutes for groups of three)*.

I'd like you to imagine that a friend would like to reduce their screen time, or the amount of time they spend on devices such as phones or tablets. Here are some ideas they are thinking about and a question for you to discuss. First you have some time to look at the task.

Place Part 3 booklet, open at Task 3, in front of the candidates. Allow 15 seconds.

Now, talk to each other about **the possible consequences of using these ways of reducing screen time.**

Candidate A

....

2 minutes (3 minutes for groups of three)

Interlocutor Thank you. Now you have about a minute to decide **which idea your friend should prioritise.**

Candidate B

....

Approximately 30 seconds

Interlocutor Thank you. (Can I have the booklet, please?) *Retrieve Part 3 booklet.*

Part 4
4 minutes (6 minutes for groups of three)

Interlocutor *Use the following questions, in order, as appropriate:*

Do you think people are aware of how much time they spend using devices? ...... (Why? / Why not?)

Some people are in favour of banning devices from classrooms because they are a distraction. Do you agree? ...... (Why?)

Why do you think people keep checking their phones or devices?

It is thought that there is a link between screen time and people's mental health. What do you think about this? ...... (Why?)

Is it realistic for most people to have regular device-free days? ...... (Why? / Why not?)

People have different opinions about whether screen addiction actually exists. What's your view? ...... (Why? / Why not?)

Select any of the following prompts, as appropriate:
- **What do you think?**
- **Do you agree?**
- **And you?**

Interlocutor Thank you. That is the end of the test.

Cambridge B2 First: Speaking

Test 4 – Part 3
Booklet

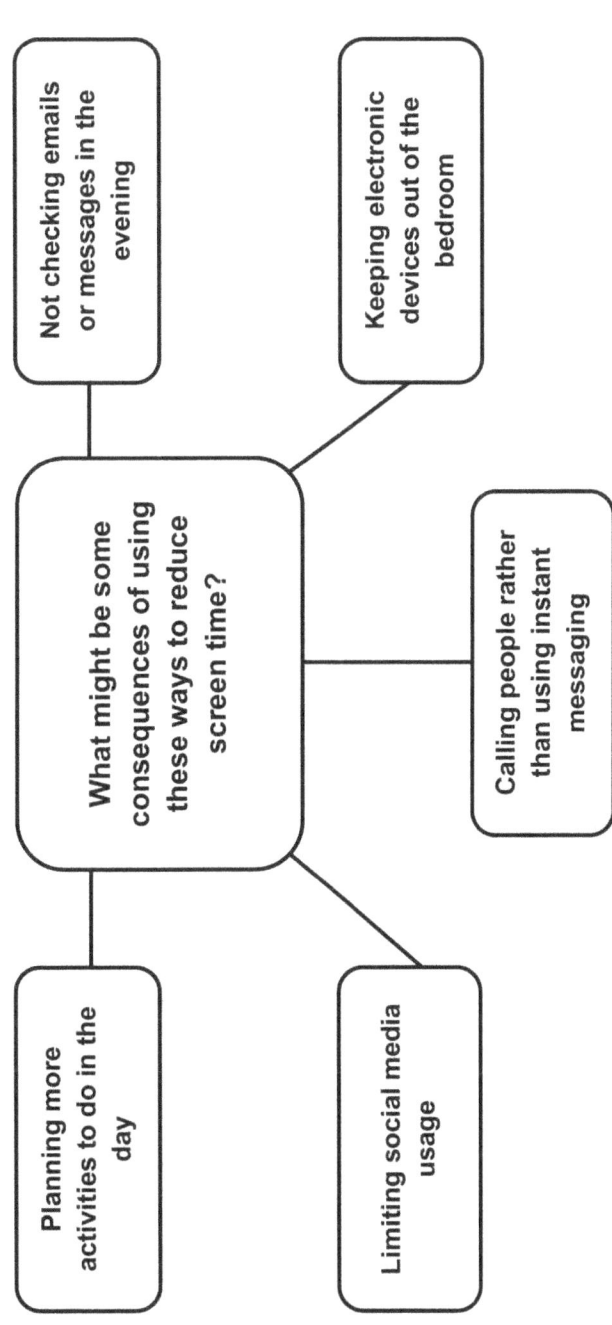

Speaking First — Mark sheet

Date | DD | MM | YY |

Candidate _____

Marks available

Grammar and vocabulary	0	1	1.5	2	2.5	3	3.5	4	4.5	5
Discourse Management	0	1	1.5	2	2.5	3	3.5	4	4.5	5
Pronunciation	0	1	1.5	2	2.5	3	3.5	4	4.5	5
Interactive Communication	0	1	1.5	2	2.5	3	3.5	4	4.5	5

Item descriptors

Grammar and vocabulary *Control* *Range*	• Degree of control of grammatical forms. • Range of grammatical forms used.
Discourse Management *Extent* *Relevance* *Coherence* *Cohesion*	• Stretches of language produced. • Relevance of contributions and organisation of ideas. • Use of appropriate cohesive devices and discourse markers.
Pronunciation *Intonation* *Stress* *Individual sounds*	• Intelligibility • Intonation • Word stress • Individual sounds
Interactive Communication *Initiating* *Responding* *Development*	• Initiating, responding and linking contributions to other speakers' interventions. • Maintaining and developing interaction, and negotiating towards an outcome.

Cambridge B2 First Speaking

Test 5

Test 5 – Part 1
2 minutes (3 minutes for groups of three)

Cambridge B2 First: Speaking

Candidates' background

Good morning/afternoon/evening. My name is …………. and this is my colleague …………. .

And your names are?

Can I have your mark sheets, please?

Thank you.

- Where are you from, *(Candidate A)*?
- And you, *(Candidate B)*?

First, we'd like to know something about you.

Select one or more questions from any of the following categories, as appropriate.

Reading

- **Tell us about a book you have enjoyed.**
- **How have your reading habits changed since childhood? …… (Why?)**
- **What do you think about graphic novels and comics? …… (Why?)**
- **How do you usually decide what to read? …… (Why?)**

Housework

- **Would you say that you do a lot of housework? …… (Why? / Why not?)**
- **What housework chore do you find the most enjoyable? …… (Why?)**
- **When did you start learning about housework chores? …… (How did you learn about them?)**
- **Would you trust robots to do your housework chores? …… (Why? / Why not?)**

Social media

- **How often do you use social media? …… (What do you use it for?)**
- **What was the last thing you posted on social media? …… (How did people respond to it?)**
- **What is the most popular social media platform in** (candidate's country)**? …… (Why?)**
- **Have you ever bought something because of social media? …… (Why? / Why not?)**

Cambridge B2 First: Speaking

Test 5 – Part 2
4 minutes (6 minutes for groups of three)

| 1 Important life milestones | 2 Important celebrations |

Interlocutor In this part of the test, I'm going to give each of you two photographs. I'd like you to talk about your photographs on your own for about a minute, and also to answer a question about your partner's photographs.

(Candidate A), it's your turn first. Here are your photographs. They show **people doing things which are important moments in life**

*Place **Part 2** booklet, open at **Task 1**, in front of Candidate A.*

I'd like you to compare the photographs, and say **how you think the people might be feeling in these situations.**

All right?

Candidate A

....
1 minute

Interlocutor Thank you.

(Candidate B), **which situation do you think is more stressful? ...... (Why?)**

Candidate B

....
Approximately 30 seconds

Interlocutor Thank you. (Can I have the booklet, please?) *Retrieve **Part 2** booklet.*

Now, *(Candidate B)*, here are your photographs. They show **people trying to sell different kinds of products.**

*Place **Part 2** booklet, open at **Task 2**, in front of Candidate B.*

I'd like you to compare the photographs, and **say what sales techniques might be important in these different situations.**

All right?

Candidate B

....
1 minute

Interlocutor Thank you.

(Candidate A), **what makes you more likely to buy something? ...... (Why?)**

Candidate A

....
Approximately 30 seconds

Interlocutor Thank you. (Can I have the booklet, please?) *Retrieve **Part 2** booklet.*

Test 5 – Part 2
Booklet 1

Cambridge B2 First: Speaking

How might the people be feeling in these situations?

Cambridge B2 First: Speaking

Test 5 – Part 2
Booklet 2

What sales techniques might be important in these different situations?

Test 5 – Part 3
4 minutes (5 minutes for groups of three)

Cambridge B2 First: Speaking

Investing in the arts

Interlocutor Now, I'd like you to talk about something together for about two minutes *(3 minutes for groups of three)*.

I'd like you to imagine that a city would like to invest some money to increase public participation in art and culture. Here are some ideas they are thinking about and a question for you to discuss. First you have some time to look at the task.

*Place **Part 3** booklet, open at **Task 3**, in front of the candidates. Allow 15 seconds.*

Now, talk to each other about **what work would be required to implement each of these measures.**

Candidate A

....
2 minutes (3 minutes for groups of three)

Interlocutor Thank you. Now you have about a minute to decide **which idea is most likely to increase participation in art and culture.**

Candidate B

....
Approximately 30 seconds

Interlocutor Thank you. (Can I have the booklet, please?) *Retrieve **Part 3** booklet.*

Part 4
4 minutes (6 minutes for groups of three)

Interlocutor *Use the following questions, in order, as appropriate:*

Select any of the following prompts, as appropriate:
• **What do you think?**
• **Do you agree?**
• **And you?**

Do you think art and culture should be a priority for a city? …… (Why? / Why not?)

Some people say that modern styles of street art should not be allowed in cities with historical architecture. Do you agree? …… (Why? / Why not?)

Do you think that art and culture are seen as things that only certain sectors of society can access? …… (Why? / Why not?)

Should galleries and museums do more to attract young people, and if so, how? …… (Why? / Why not?)

What role does the internet play in art and culture? …… (Why?)

Some people say that art has the power to change the world. What's your view? …… (Why?)

Interlocutor Thank you. That is the end of the test.

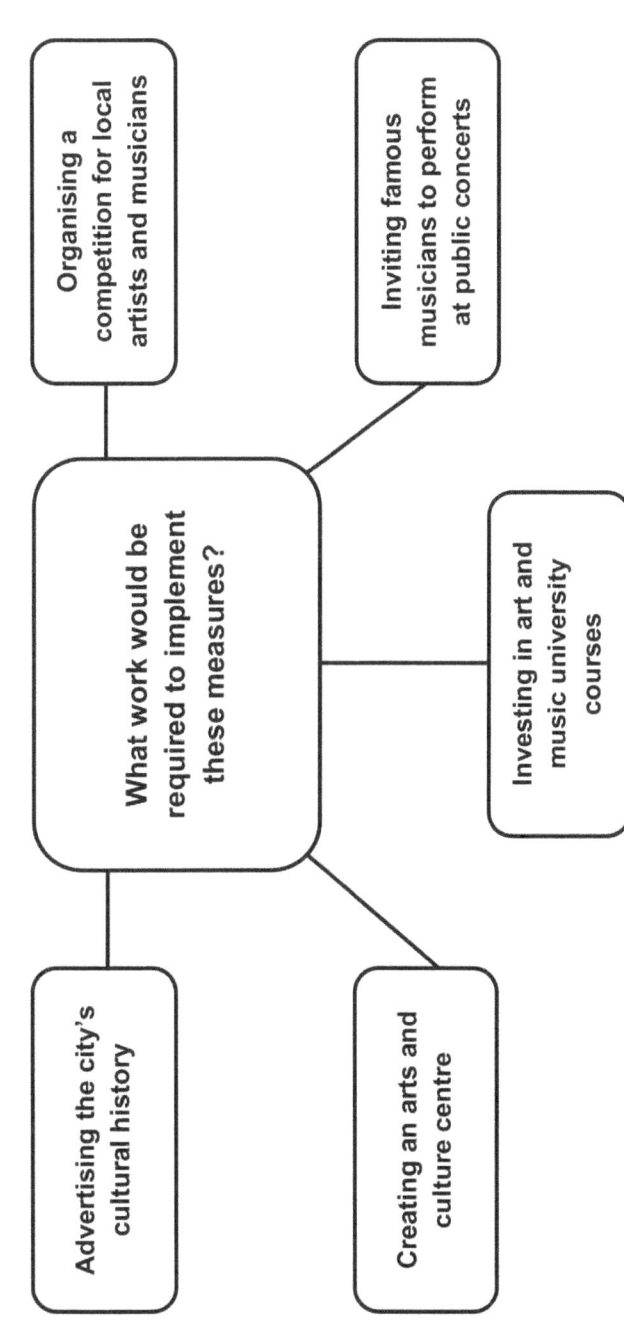

Speaking First — Mark sheet

Date | DD | MM | YY |

Candidate _____

Marks available

Grammar and vocabulary	0	1	1.5	2	2.5	3	3.5	4	4.5	5
Discourse Management	0	1	1.5	2	2.5	3	3.5	4	4.5	5
Pronunciation	0	1	1.5	2	2.5	3	3.5	4	4.5	5
Interactive Communication	0	1	1.5	2	2.5	3	3.5	4	4.5	5

Item descriptors

Grammar and vocabulary *Control* *Range*	• Degree of control of grammatical forms. • Range of grammatical forms used.
Discourse Management *Extent* *Relevance* *Coherence* *Cohesion*	• Stretches of language produced. • Relevance of contributions and organisation of ideas. • Use of appropriate cohesive devices and discourse markers.
Pronunciation *Intonation* *Stress* *Individual sounds*	• Intelligibility • Intonation • Word stress • Individual sounds
Interactive Communication *Initiating* *Responding* *Development*	• Initiating, responding and linking contributions to other speakers' interventions. • Maintaining and developing interaction, and negotiating towards an outcome.

Cambridge B2 First Speaking

Test 6

Test 6 – Part 1
2 minutes (3 minutes for groups of three)

Cambridge B2 First: Speaking

Candidates' background

Good morning/afternoon/evening. My name is …………… and this is my colleague …………… .

And your names are?

Can I have your mark sheets, please?

Thank you.

- Where are you from, *(Candidate A)*?
- And you, *(Candidate B)*?

First, we'd like to know something about you.

Select one or more questions from any of the following categories, as appropriate.

TV gameshows and quiz shows

- **How often do you watch TV gameshows or TV quiz shows?** …… **(Why?)**
- **Tell us about a show that is popular in** (candidate's country). …… **(Why is it popular?)**
- **What type of puzzles or quizzes do you like doing?** …… **(Why?)**
- **Do you prefer team or individual puzzles?** …… **(Why?)**

Homes and neighbours

- **What type of building is your home?** …… **(Tell us about it.)**
- **If you could live in a different type of home, what type would you choose?** …… **(Why?)**
- **Would you describe yourself as a good neighbour?** …… **(Why? / Why not?)**
- **In your opinion, how important is it to get on with your neighbours?** …… **(Why?)**

Pets

- **Have you ever had any pets?** …… **(Tell us about it/one of them.)**
- **Do you think you'll have** (a / another) **pet in the future?** …… **(Why? / Why not?)**
- **What makes a good pet owner?** …… **(Why?)**
- **What type of animals do you like the most?** …… **(Why?)**

Cambridge B2 First: Speaking

Test 6 – Part 2
4 minutes (6 minutes for groups of three)

| 1 Learning about the past | 2 Robots |

Interlocutor In this part of the test, I'm going to give each of you two photographs. I'd like you to talk about your photographs on your own for about a minute, and also to answer a question about your partner's photographs.

(Candidate A), it's your turn first. Here are your photographs. They show **people learning about the past in different ways**.

*Place **Part 2** booklet, open at **Task 1**, in front of Candidate A.*

I'd like you to compare the photographs, and say **what you think the people can gain from learning about the past in these ways.**

All right?

Candidate A

....

1 minute

Interlocutor Thank you.

(Candidate B), **do you find it interesting to learn about the past? ...... (Why? / Why not?)**

Candidate B

....

Approximately 30 seconds

Interlocutor Thank you. (Can I have the booklet, please?) *Retrieve **Part 2** booklet.*

Now, *(Candidate B)*, here are your photographs. They show **people interacting with robots in different situations**.

*Place **Part 2** booklet, open at **Task 2**, in front of Candidate B.*

I'd like you to compare the photographs, and say **how beneficial robots are in these situations.**

All right?

Candidate B

....

1 minute

Interlocutor Thank you.

(Candidate A), **Would you like to use robots in your daily life? ...... (Why? / Why not?)**

Candidate A

....

Approximately 30 seconds

Interlocutor Thank you. (Can I have the booklet, please?) *Retrieve **Part 2** booklet.*

What can people gain from learning about the past in these ways?

Cambridge B2 First: Speaking

Test 6 – Part 2
Booklet 2

How beneficial are robots in these situations?

Test 6 – Part 3
4 minutes (5 minutes for groups of three)

Cambridge B2 First: Speaking

Marketing a soft drink

Interlocutor Now, I'd like you to talk about something together for about two minutes *(3 minutes for groups of three)*.

I'd like you to imagine that a company is preparing to launch a new soft drink and wants to find ways to make people aware of the product. Here are some ideas they are thinking about and a question for you to discuss. First you have some time to look at the task.

*Place **Part 3** booklet, open at **Task 3**, in front of the candidates. Allow 15 seconds.*

Now, talk to each other about **the potential pros and cons of these ideas for the company.**

Candidate A

....
2 minutes (3 minutes for groups of three)

Interlocutor Thank you. Now you have about a minute to decide **which idea would be the best for the company.**

Candidate B

....
Approximately 30 seconds

Interlocutor Thank you. (Can I have the booklet, please?) *Retrieve **Part 3** booklet.*

Part 4
4 minutes (6 minutes for groups of three)

Interlocutor *Use the following questions, in order, as appropriate:*

Select any of the following prompts, as appropriate:
• **What do you think?**
• **Do you agree?**
• **And you?**

What can be done to prevent children from being exposed to advertising? …… **(Is it important to do this?)**

Some people are concerned that social media advertising can be particularly harmful. Do you agree? …… **(Why? / Why not?)**

How are soft drinks usually advertised in (candidate's country)? …… **(Why?)**

Do you think that mentioning price is a good idea when advertising big items like cars? …… **(Why? / Why not?)**

Some people claim that their shopping habits are not influenced by advertising. What do you think? (Why? / Why not?)

Do you think it is more important for a company to have good customer service or great products? …… **(Why?)**

Interlocutor Thank you. That is the end of the test.

Cambridge B2 First: Speaking

Test 6 – Part 3
Booklet

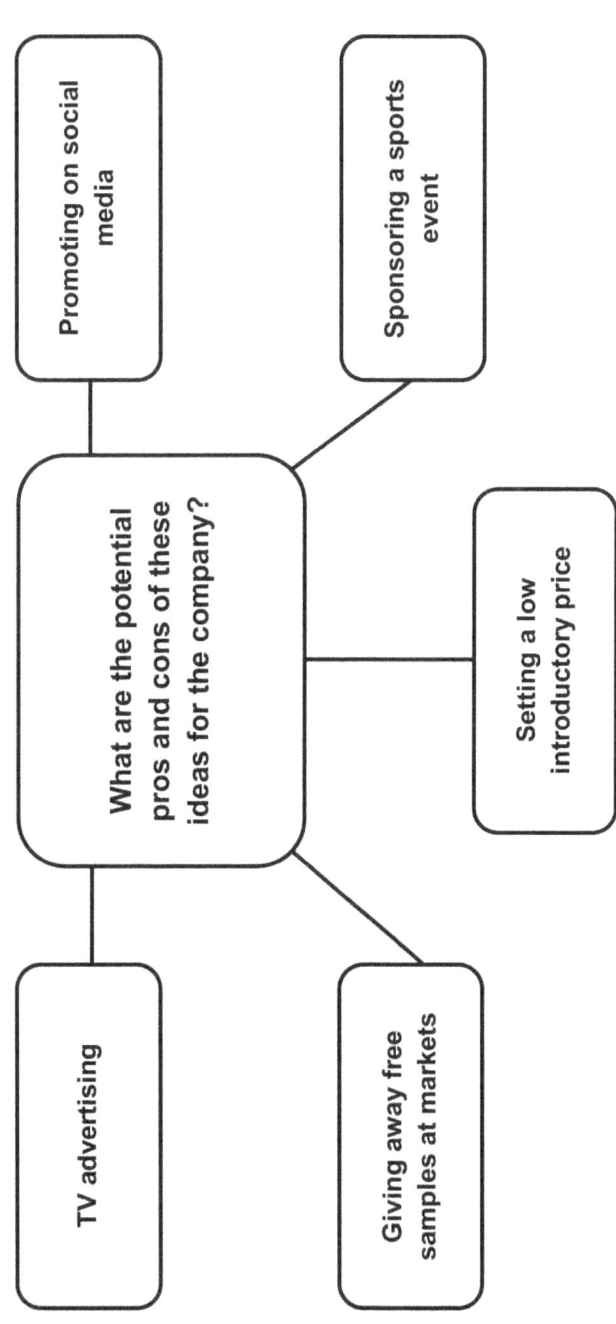

Speaking First — Mark sheet

Date | DD | MM | YY |

Candidate _____

Marks available

Grammar and vocabulary	0	1	1.5	2	2.5	3	3.5	4	4.5	5
Discourse Management	0	1	1.5	2	2.5	3	3.5	4	4.5	5
Pronunciation	0	1	1.5	2	2.5	3	3.5	4	4.5	5
Interactive Communication	0	1	1.5	2	2.5	3	3.5	4	4.5	5

Item descriptors

Grammar and vocabulary *Control* *Range*	• Degree of control of grammatical forms. • Range of grammatical forms used.
Discourse Management *Extent* *Relevance* *Coherence* *Cohesion*	• Stretches of language produced. • Relevance of contributions and organisation of ideas. • Use of appropriate cohesive devices and discourse markers.
Pronunciation *Intonation* *Stress* *Individual sounds*	• Intelligibility • Intonation • Word stress • Individual sounds
Interactive Communication *Initiating* *Responding* *Development*	• Initiating, responding and linking contributions to other speakers' interventions. • Maintaining and developing interaction, and negotiating towards an outcome.

Cambridge B2 First Speaking

Test 7

Test 7 – Part 1	Cambridge B2 First: Speaking
2 minutes (3 minutes for groups of three)	

Candidates' background

Good morning/afternoon/evening. My name is …………… and this is my colleague …………… .

And your names are?

Can I have your mark sheets, please?

Thank you.

- Where are you from, *(Candidate A)*?
- And you, *(Candidate B)*?

First, we'd like to know something about you.

Select one or more questions from any of the following categories, as appropriate.

Nature

- **What is the countryside like in** (candidate's country)**?**
- **When was the last time you spent time in nature? …… (Tell us about it.)**
- **How often do you spend time in nature? …… (Why?)**
- **What type of natural landscape do you prefer? …… (Why?)**

Weekends

- **What did you do last weekend?**
- **How has the way you spend weekends changed over the years? …… (Why?)**
- **Would you rather make lots of plans for the weekend or relax at home? …… (Why?)**
- **How would you feel if your boss asked you to work at weekends? …… (Why?)**

Photography

- **Do you like taking photographs? …… (What type of pictures do you take?)**
- **Would you say you take good pictures? …… (Why? / Why not?)**
- **How often do you share your photos on social media? …… (Why do you like it?)**
- **Have you ever taken a photography class? …… (What did you learn? / Would you like to?)**

Cambridge B2 First: Speaking

Test 7 – Part 2
4 minutes (6 minutes for groups of three)

| 1 Neighbours | 2 Spending time together |

Interlocutor In this part of the test, I'm going to give each of you two photographs. I'd like you to talk about your photographs on your own for about a minute, and also to answer a question about your partner's photographs.

(Candidate A), it's your turn first. Here are your photographs. They show **people who have different types of relationship with their neighbours**.

*Place **Part 2** booklet, open at **Task 1**, in front of Candidate A.*

I'd like you to compare the photographs, and say **how the people might be feeling in these situations.**

All right?

Candidate A

....
1 minute

Interlocutor Thank you.

(Candidate B), **do you think you are a good neighbour? …… (Why? / Why not?)**

Candidate B

....
Approximately 30 seconds

Interlocutor Thank you. (Can I have the booklet, please?) *Retrieve **Part 2** booklet.*

Now, *(Candidate B)*, here are your photographs. They show **relatives spending time together in different ways**.

*Place **Part 2** booklet, open at **Task 2**, in front of Candidate B.*

I'd like you to compare the photographs, and say **what you think the people are enjoying about spending time together in these ways.**

All right?

Candidate B

....
1 minute

Interlocutor Thank you.

(Candidate A), **which activity would you prefer to do with your family? …… (Why?)**

Candidate A

....
Approximately 30 seconds

Interlocutor Thank you. (Can I have the booklet, please?) *Retrieve **Part 2** booklet.*

Test 7 – Part 2
Booklet 1

Cambridge B2 First: Speaking

How might the people be feeling in these situations?

Cambridge B2 First: Speaking

Test 7 – Part 2
Booklet 2

What are the people enjoying about spending time together in these ways?

Test 7 – Part 3
4 minutes (5 minutes for groups of three)

Cambridge B2 First: Speaking

Starting a fashion blog

Interlocutor Now, I'd like you to talk about something together for about two minutes *(3 minutes for groups of three)*.

I'd like you to imagine that a fashion company is thinking of starting a blog to help promote their brand. Here are some topics they are thinking about for their first blog post and a question for you to discuss. First you have some time to look at the task.

Place Part 3 booklet, open at Task 3, in front of the candidates. Allow 15 seconds.

Now, talk to each other about **who would be most likely to find these topics interesting.**

Candidate A

....

2 minutes (3 minutes for groups of three)

Interlocutor Thank you. Now you have about a minute to decide **which idea would be the best for the first blog post.**

Candidate B

....

Approximately 30 seconds

Interlocutor Thank you. (Can I have the booklet, please?) *Retrieve Part 3 booklet.*

Part 4
4 minutes (6 minutes for groups of three)

Interlocutor *Use the following questions, in order, as appropriate:*

Apart from the subject, what makes a good blog post? ...... (Why?)
How do retail companies benefit from having blogs? ...... (Why?)

Select any of the following prompts, as appropriate:
- **What do you think?**
- **Do you agree?**
- **And you?**

Is fashion an important sector in (candidate's country)? ...... (Why? / Why not?)

How do fashion companies use psychology to promote their clothes?

Some people believe that consumers have the power to make the fashion industry more environmentally responsible. Do you agree? ...... (Why? / Why not?)

What have been the main advantages and disadvantages of globalisation in the fashion industry?

Interlocutor Thank you. That is the end of the test.

Cambridge B2 First: Speaking

Test 7 – Part 3
Booklet

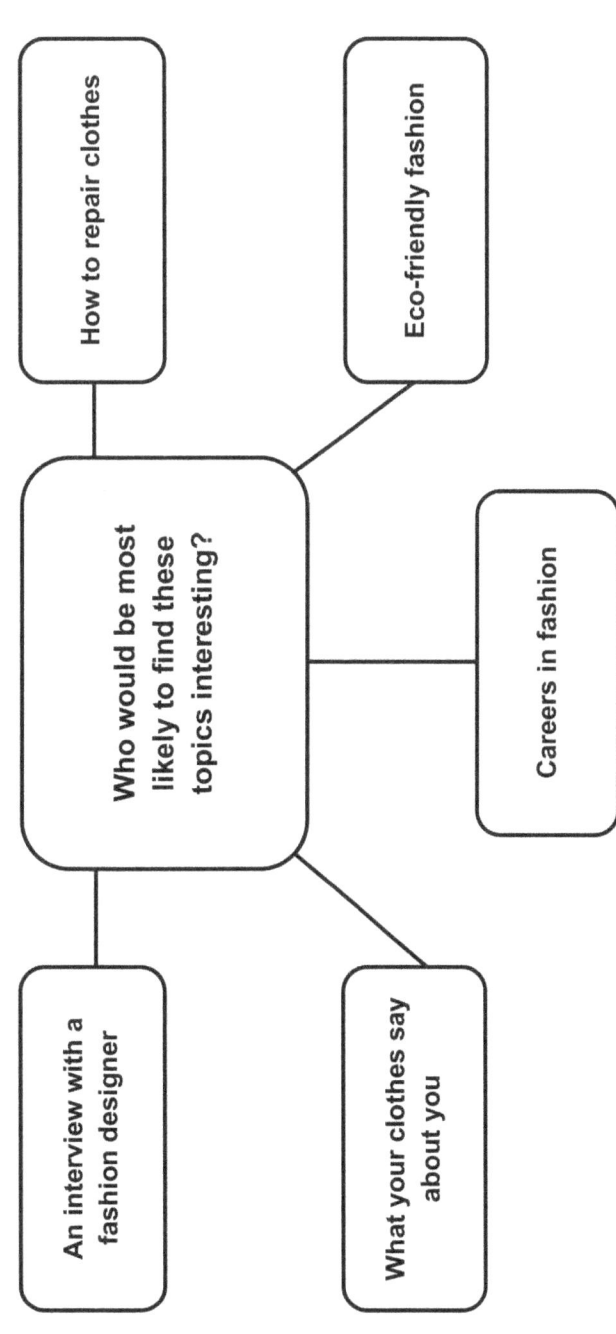

Speaking First — Mark sheet

Date | DD | MM | YY |

Candidate _____

Marks available

Grammar and vocabulary	0	1	1.5	2	2.5	3	3.5	4	4.5	5
Discourse Management	0	1	1.5	2	2.5	3	3.5	4	4.5	5
Pronunciation	0	1	1.5	2	2.5	3	3.5	4	4.5	5
Interactive Communication	0	1	1.5	2	2.5	3	3.5	4	4.5	5

Item descriptors

Grammar and vocabulary *Control* *Range*	• Degree of control of grammatical forms. • Range of grammatical forms used.
Discourse Management *Extent* *Relevance* *Coherence* *Cohesion*	• Stretches of language produced. • Relevance of contributions and organisation of ideas. • Use of appropriate cohesive devices and discourse markers.
Pronunciation *Intonation* *Stress* *Individual sounds*	• Intelligibility • Intonation • Word stress • Individual sounds
Interactive Communication *Initiating* *Responding* *Development*	• Initiating, responding and linking contributions to other speakers' interventions. • Maintaining and developing interaction, and negotiating towards an outcome.

Cambridge B2 First Speaking

Test 8

Test 8 – Part 1
2 minutes (3 minutes for groups of three)

Cambridge B2 First: Speaking

Candidates' background

Good morning/afternoon/evening. My name is .... and this is my colleague ....

And your names are?

Can I have your mark sheets, please?

Thank you.

- Where are you from, *(Candidate A)*?
- And you, *(Candidate B)*?

First, we'd like to know something about you.

Select one or more questions from any of the following categories, as appropriate.

Seasons

- **Tell us about the different seasons in** (candidate's country).
- **What is your favourite time of year? ...... (Why?)**
- **Would you like to live in a place with one season all year? ...... (Why? / Why not?)**
- **How much do changes in the seasons affect your daily routine? ...... (Why?)**

Transport and driving

- **Can you describe public transport in the place where you live? ...... (Do you use it?)**
- **What is your preferred way to travel? ...... (Why?)**
- **Is getting a driving licence difficult in** (candidate's country)? **...... (What do you think about that?)**
- **What would you change about transport in your country? ...... (Why?)**

Toys and games

- **Tell us about a favourite toy or game you liked from your childhood. ...... (Why did you like it?)**
- **Do you think playing games helped you to develop? ...... (How? / Why not?)**
- **Have you kept any toys that you used to play with? ...... (Why? / Why not?)**
- **If you had to buy a toy for a child now, which one would you choose? ...... (Why?)**

Cambridge B2 First: Speaking

Test 8 – Part 2
4 minutes (6 minutes for groups of three)

1 Ways of communicating	2 Dancing

Interlocutor In this part of the test, I'm going to give each of you two photographs. I'd like you to talk about your photographs on your own for about a minute, and also to answer a question about your partner's photographs.

(Candidate A), it's your turn first. Here are your photographs. They show **people communicating in different ways**.

*Place **Part 2** booklet, open at **Task 1**, in front of Candidate A.*

I'd like you to compare the photographs, and say **why you think the people have chosen to communicate in these ways**.

All right?

Candidate A

....

1 minute

Interlocutor Thank you.

(Candidate B), **which form of communication do you use most often? …… (Why?)**

Candidate B

....

Approximately 30 seconds

Interlocutor Thank you. (Can I have the booklet, please?) *Retrieve **Part 2** booklet.*

Now, *(Candidate B)*, here are your photographs. They show **people learning to do different types of dance**.

*Place **Part 2** booklet, open at **Task 2**, in front of Candidate B.*

I'd like you to compare the photographs, and **say how much physical skill these types of dancing require.**

All right?

Candidate B

....

1 minute

Interlocutor Thank you.

(Candidate A), **which type of dance would you rather do? …… (Why?)**

Candidate A

....

Approximately 30 seconds

Interlocutor Thank you. (Can I have the booklet, please?) *Retrieve **Part 2** booklet.*

Test 8 – Part 2
Booklet 1

Cambridge B2 First: Speaking

Why have the people chosen to communicate in these ways?

Cambridge B2 First: Speaking

Test 8 – Part 2
Booklet 2

How much physical skill do these types of dancing require?

Test 8 – Part 3
4 minutes (5 minutes for groups of three)

Cambridge B2 First: Speaking

Choosing a speaker

Interlocutor Now, I'd like you to talk about something together for about two minutes *(3 minutes for groups of three)*.

I'd like you to imagine that a school is planning to invite a speaker to give a talk to pupils aged 14–16. Here are some people they are thinking about inviting and a question for you to discuss. First you have some time to look at the task.

Place Part 3 booklet, open at Task 3, in front of the candidates. Allow 15 seconds.

Now, talk to each other about **how these people might inspire students.**

Candidate A

....

2 minutes (3 minutes for groups of three)

Interlocutor Thank you. Now you have about a minute to decide **which speaker would be the best for the school.**

Candidate B

....

Approximately 30 seconds

Interlocutor Thank you. (Can I have the booklet, please?) *Retrieve Part 3 booklet.*

Part 4
4 minutes (6 minutes for groups of three)

Interlocutor *Use the following questions, in order, as appropriate:*

> *Select any of the following prompts, as appropriate:*
> - **What do you think?**
> - **Do you agree?**
> - **And you?**

What should presenters do to make their talks interesting? …… (Why?)

Why might students prefer a live presentation instead of watching an online video?

What is an appropriate age for students to start planning their future? …… (Why?)

What should schools be doing to help students prepare for their future? …… (Why?) …… (How?)Some people say that celebrities receive too much attention in society, and that they do not make good role models. Do you agree? …… (Why? / Why not?)

Some people say that schools should arrange some kind of work experience for students. Do you agree? …… (Why? / Why not?)

Interlocutor Thank you. That is the end of the test.

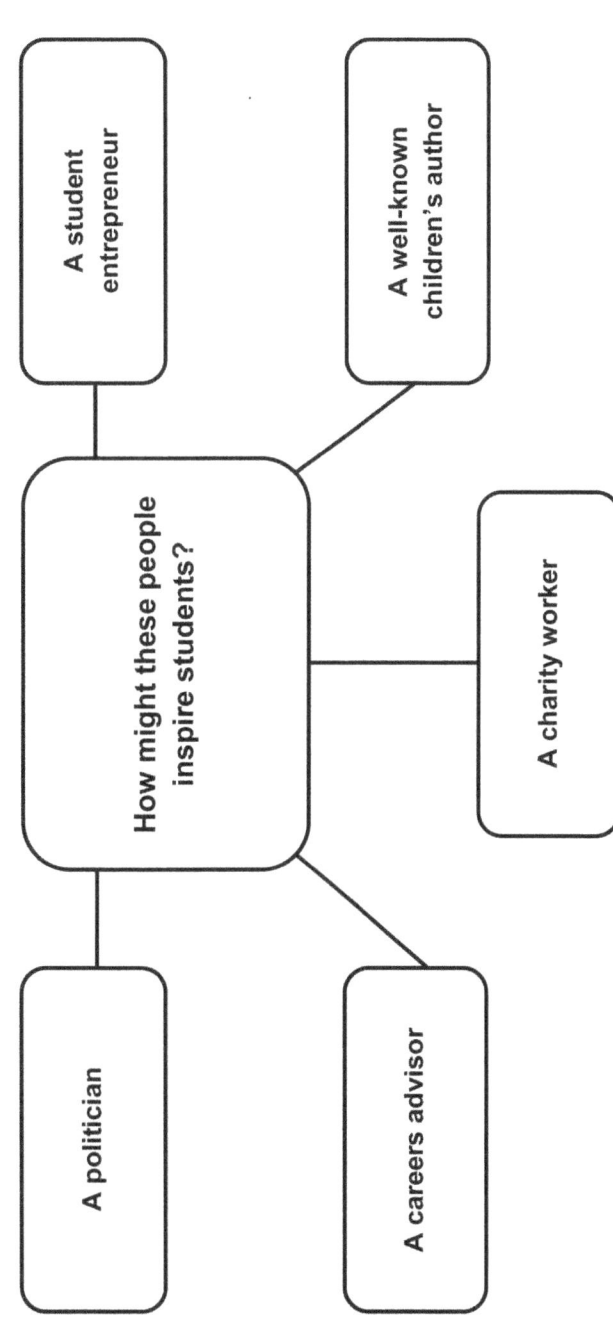

Speaking First — Mark sheet

Date | DD | MM | YY |

Candidate _____

Marks available

Grammar and vocabulary	0	1	1.5	2	2.5	3	3.5	4	4.5	5
Discourse Management	0	1	1.5	2	2.5	3	3.5	4	4.5	5
Pronunciation	0	1	1.5	2	2.5	3	3.5	4	4.5	5
Interactive Communication	0	1	1.5	2	2.5	3	3.5	4	4.5	5

Item descriptors

Grammar and vocabulary *Control* *Range*	• Degree of control of grammatical forms. • Range of grammatical forms used.
Discourse Management *Extent* *Relevance* *Coherence* *Cohesion*	• Stretches of language produced. • Relevance of contributions and organisation of ideas. • Use of appropriate cohesive devices and discourse markers.
Pronunciation *Intonation* *Stress* *Individual sounds*	• Intelligibility • Intonation • Word stress • Individual sounds
Interactive Communication *Initiating* *Responding* *Development*	• Initiating, responding and linking contributions to other speakers' interventions. • Maintaining and developing interaction, and negotiating towards an outcome.

Cambridge B2 First Speaking

Test 9

Test 9 – Part 1
2 minutes (3 minutes for groups of three)

Cambridge B2 First: Speaking

Candidates' background

Good morning/afternoon/evening. My name is .... and this is my colleague ....

And your names are?

Can I have your mark sheets, please?

Thank you.

- Where are you from, *(Candidate A)*?
- And you, *(Candidate B)*?

First, we'd like to know something about you.

Select one or more questions from any of the following categories, as appropriate.

TV

- **What types of TV show do you enjoy? ...... (Why?)**
- **Tell us about some popular TV shows in** (candidate's country).
- **When was the last time you were really affected by a TV show? ...... (Tell us about it.)**
- **How much TV do you watch in a typical week? ...... (Is this the right amount for you? ...... Why?)**

Future plans

- **What are you going to do next weekend?**
- **Are you someone who likes making plans in advance? ...... (Why? Why not?)**
- **How would you feel if someone suddenly wanted you to change your plans? ...... (Why?)**
- **What plans do you have for the future? ...... (What will you need to do to achieve them?)**

Celebrities

- **Tell us about some celebrities from** (candidate's country). **...... (What do you think about them?)**
- **Which famous people inspired or influenced you when you were younger? ...... (Why?)**
- **Do you like reading about the lives of celebrities? ...... (Why? Why not?)**
- **If you could interview any celebrity, who would you choose? ...... (What would you ask them?)**

Cambridge B2 First: Speaking

Test 9 – Part 2
4 minutes (6 minutes for groups of three)

| 1 Making decisions | 2 Being at home |

Interlocutor In this part of the test, I'm going to give each of you two photographs. I'd like you to talk about your photographs on your own for about a minute, and also to answer a question about your partner's photographs.

(Candidate A), it's your turn first. Here are your photographs. They show **people making decisions in different situations**.

Place Part 2 booklet, open at Task 1, in front of Candidate A.

I'd like you to compare the photographs, and say **how important it is to get advice from others when making these decisions.**

All right?

Candidate A

....
1 minute

Interlocutor Thank you.

(Candidate B), **do you feel confident making important decisions? …… (Why? / Why not?)**

Candidate B

....
Approximately 30 seconds

Interlocutor Thank you. (Can I have the booklet, please?) *Retrieve Part 2 booklet.*

Now, *(Candidate B)*, here are your photographs. They show **people spending time at home in different ways**.

Place Part 2 booklet, open at Task 2, in front of Candidate B.

I'd like you to compare the photographs, and say **how the people might be feeling about being at home.**

All right?

Candidate B

....
1 minute

Interlocutor Thank you.

(Candidate A), **do you prefer entertaining people at your home or visiting their home? …… (Why?)**

Candidate A

....
Approximately 30 seconds

Interlocutor Thank you. (Can I have the booklet, please?) *Retrieve Part 2 booklet.*

Test 9 – Part 2
Booklet 1

Cambridge B2 First: Speaking

How important is it to get advice from others in these situations?

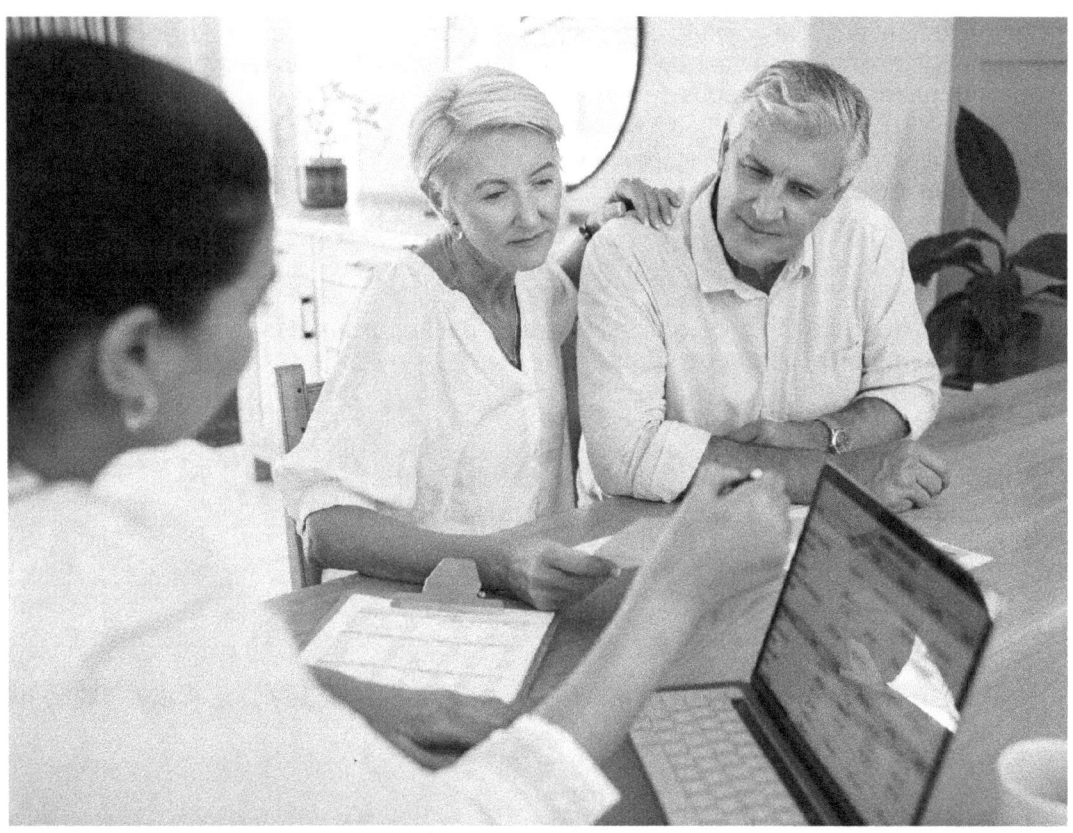

Cambridge B2 First: Speaking

Test 9 – Part 2
Booklet 2

How might the people be feeling about being at home?

Test 9 – Part 3
4 minutes (5 minutes for groups of three)

Cambridge B2 First: Speaking

Most charming town

Interlocutor Now, I'd like you to talk about something together for about two minutes *(3 minutes for groups of three)*.

I'd like you to imagine that a town is preparing to enter a national competition called "most charming town". To improve its chances of winning, it has called a meeting to hear local people's suggestions. Here are some ideas that will be discussed in the meeting and a question for you to discuss. First you have some time to look at the task.

Place Part 3 booklet, open at Task 3, in front of the candidates. Allow 15 seconds.

Now, talk to each other about **how these issues may affect local residents.**

Candidate A

....
2 minutes (3 minutes for groups of three)

Interlocutor Thank you. Now you have about a minute to decide **which issue should be prioritised to improve the town's chances of winning the competition.**

Candidate B

....
Approximately 30 seconds

Interlocutor Thank you. (Can I have the booklet, please?) *Retrieve Part 3 booklet.*

Part 4
4 minutes (6 minutes for groups of three)

Interlocutor *Use the following questions, in order, as appropriate:*

Select any of the following prompts, as appropriate:
- **What do you think?**
- **Do you agree?**
- **And you?**

Some people view public meetings as a waste of time. What do you think? …… (Why?)

What are the most effective ways that local residents can make their views heard? …… (Why?)

Some people argue that competitions like "most charming town" are more about boosting tourism than improving things for residents. Do you agree? …… (Why? / Why not?)

In your opinion, does tourism make a place more or less charming? …… (Why?)

How important is it for people to feel proud of the place where they live? (Why?)

Do you think towns should protect traditional or historical buildings if it costs a lot of money? …… (Why? / Why not?)

Interlocutor Thank you. That is the end of the test.

Cambridge B2 First: Speaking

Test 9 – Part 3
Booklet

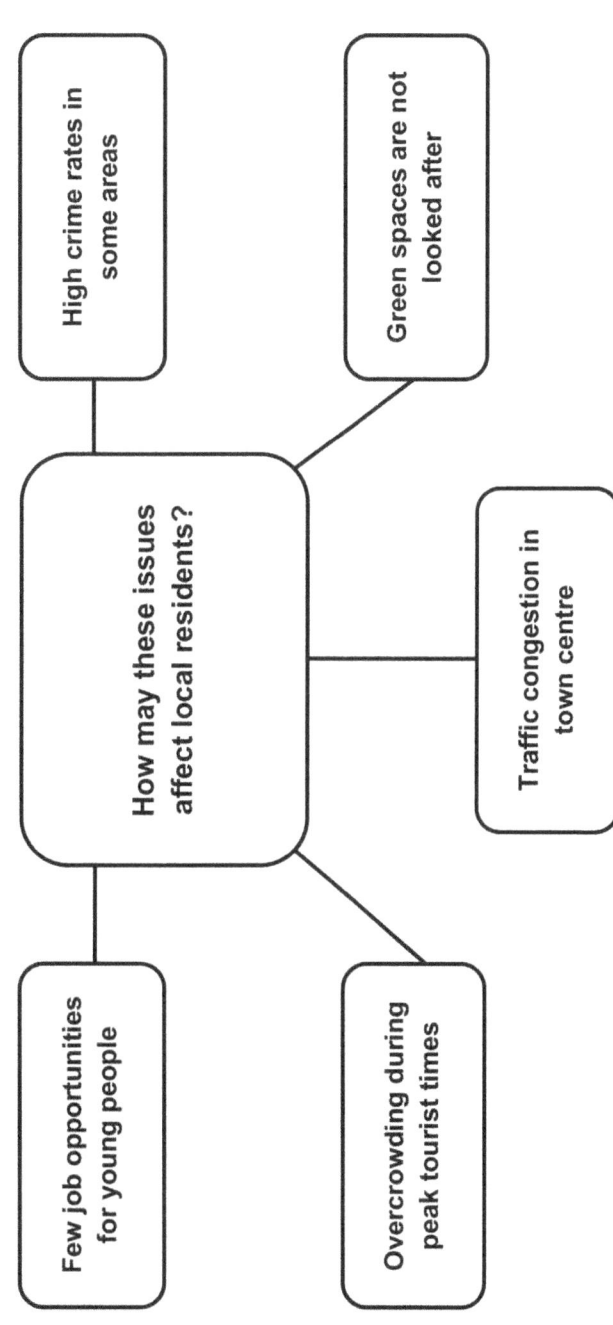

How may these issues affect local residents?

- High crime rates in some areas
- Green spaces are not looked after
- Traffic congestion in town centre
- Overcrowding during peak tourist times
- Few job opportunities for young people

Speaking First — Mark sheet

Date | DD | MM | YY |

Candidate _____

Marks available

Grammar and vocabulary	0	1	1.5	2	2.5	3	3.5	4	4.5	5
Discourse Management	0	1	1.5	2	2.5	3	3.5	4	4.5	5
Pronunciation	0	1	1.5	2	2.5	3	3.5	4	4.5	5
Interactive Communication	0	1	1.5	2	2.5	3	3.5	4	4.5	5

Item descriptors

Grammar and vocabulary *Control* *Range*	• Degree of control of grammatical forms. • Range of grammatical forms used.
Discourse Management *Extent* *Relevance* *Coherence* *Cohesion*	• Stretches of language produced. • Relevance of contributions and organisation of ideas. • Use of appropriate cohesive devices and discourse markers.
Pronunciation *Intonation* *Stress* *Individual sounds*	• Intelligibility • Intonation • Word stress • Individual sounds
Interactive Communication *Initiating* *Responding* *Development*	• Initiating, responding and linking contributions to other speakers' interventions. • Maintaining and developing interaction, and negotiating towards an outcome.

Cambridge B2 First Speaking

Test 10

Test 10 – Part 1
2 minutes (3 minutes for groups of three)

Cambridge B2 First: Speaking

Candidates' background

Good morning/afternoon/evening. My name is …………… and this is my colleague …………… .

And your names are?

Can I have your mark sheets, please?

Thank you.

- Where are you from, *(Candidate A)*?
- And you, *(Candidate B)*?

First, we'd like to know something about you.

Select one or more questions from any of the following categories, as appropriate.

Celebrations

- **When was the last time you celebrated something? …… (How did you celebrate it?)**
- **Tell us about a traditional celebration or festival in** (candidate's country).
- **How do you like to celebrate special occasions? …… (Why?)**
- **Are gifts important to you when you're celebrating a special occasion? …… (Why? / Why not?)**

Saving and spending money

- **Tell us about a recent shopping trip. …… (What did you buy?)**
- **Would you describe yourself as a spender or saver when it comes to money? …… (Why?)**
- **Is there anything about your spending habits you'd like to change? …… (Why? / Why not?)**
- **If you received a large sum of money, what would you do with it? …… (Why?)**

Education

- **Tell us about a teacher or course that has inspired you.**
- **What subjects are you most interested in? …… (Why?)**
- **What are your strengths as a student? …… (Why?)**
- **Are there any subjects you wish you could have studied at school? …… (Why? / Why not?)**

Cambridge B2 First: Speaking	Test 10 – Part 2
	4 minutes (6 minutes for groups of three)

1 Fans and hobbies	2 Cooking

Interlocutor In this part of the test, I'm going to give each of you two photographs. I'd like you to talk about your photographs on your own for about a minute, and also to answer a question about your partner's photographs.

(Candidate A), it's your turn first. Here are your photographs. They show **young people enjoying their hobby**.

*Place **Part 2** booklet, open at **Task 1**, in front of Candidate A.*

I'd like you to compare the photographs, and say **what you think the people gain from their hobby**.

All right?

Candidate A

....

1 minute

Interlocutor Thank you.

(Candidate B), **is it important that your friends have the same interests as you? ...... (Why? / Why not?)**

Candidate B

....

Approximately 30 seconds

Interlocutor Thank you. (Can I have the booklet, please?) *Retrieve **Part 2** booklet.*

Now, *(Candidate B)*, here are your photographs. They show **people cooking in different ways**.

*Place **Part 2** booklet, open at **Task 2**, in front of Candidate B.*

I'd like you to compare the photographs, and say **why the people might have decided to cook in these ways.**

All right?

Candidate B

....

1 minute

Interlocutor Thank you.

(Candidate A), **how would you feel if you had to cook for a lot of people? ...... (Why?)**

Candidate A

....

Approximately 30 seconds

Interlocutor Thank you. (Can I have the booklet, please?) *Retrieve **Part 2** booklet.*

What might the people gain from their hobby?

Cambridge B2 First: Speaking

Test 10 – Part 2
Booklet 2

Why might the people have chosen to cook in these ways?

Test 10 – Part 3
4 minutes (5 minutes for groups of three)

Cambridge B2 First: Speaking

Working and studying

Interlocutor Now, I'd like you to talk about something together for about two minutes *(3 minutes for groups of three).*

I'd like you to imagine that a student in the final year of their course is trying to decide whether to get a part-time job. Here are some factors they are considering and a question for you to discuss. First you have some time to look at the task.

*Place **Part 3** booklet, open at **Task 3**, in front of the candidates. Allow 15 seconds.*

Now, talk to each other about **how much influence each of these factors should have when deciding whether to find part-time work.**

Candidate A

2 minutes (3 minutes for groups of three)

Interlocutor Thank you. Now you have about a minute to decide **whether the student should take on work during their studies.**

Candidate B

Approximately 30 seconds

Interlocutor Thank you. (Can I have the booklet, please?) *Retrieve **Part 3** booklet.*

Part 4
4 minutes (6 minutes for groups of three)

Interlocutor *Use the following questions, in order, as appropriate:*

What are the most common part-time jobs for students in (candidate's country)? …… **(Why?)**

Select any of the following prompts, as appropriate:
- What do you think?
- Do you agree?
- And you?

Should colleges prevent students from getting part-time work? ……
(Why? / Why not?)Do you think that technology offers students more work opportunities? …… (Why? / Why not?)

Some people say that part-time work experience can help students in the future. What do you think? …… (Why?)

How might studying online affect a student's decision to take on part-time work?

Interlocutor Thank you. That is the end of the test.

Cambridge B2 First: Speaking

Test 10 – Part 3
Booklet

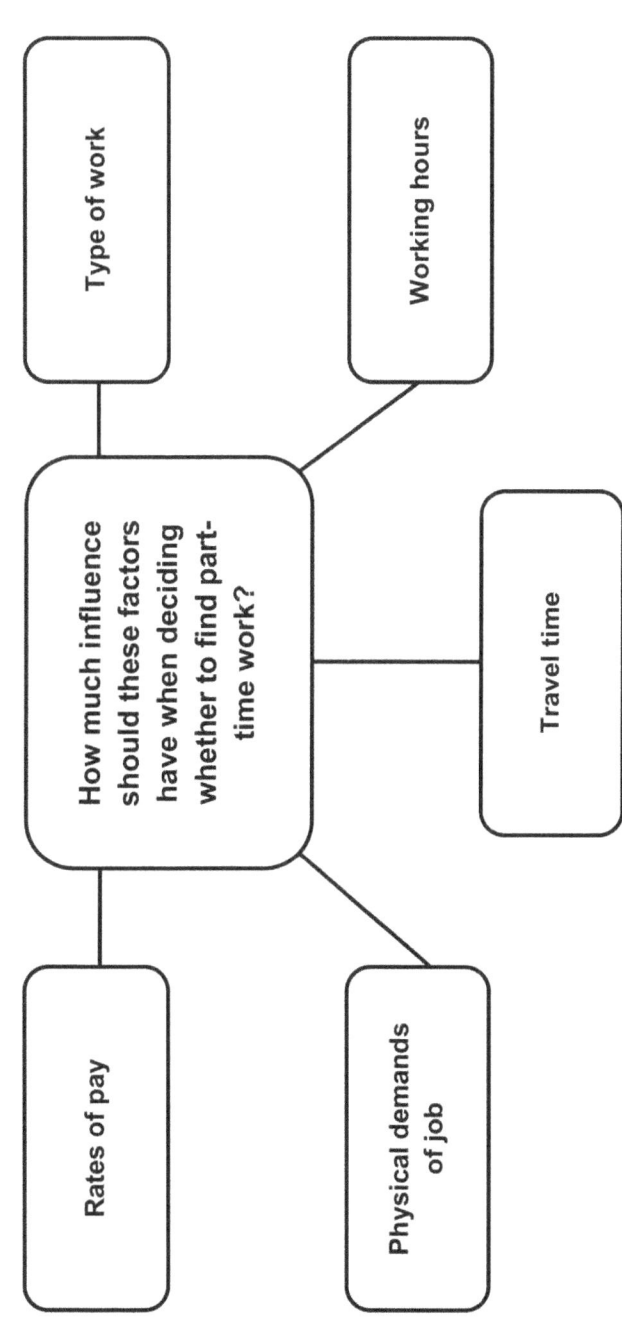

Speaking First — Mark sheet

Date | DD | MM | YY |

Candidate _____

Marks available

Grammar and vocabulary	0	1	1.5	2	2.5	3	3.5	4	4.5	5
Discourse Management	0	1	1.5	2	2.5	3	3.5	4	4.5	5
Pronunciation	0	1	1.5	2	2.5	3	3.5	4	4.5	5
Interactive Communication	0	1	1.5	2	2.5	3	3.5	4	4.5	5

Item descriptors

Grammar and vocabulary *Control* *Range*	• Degree of control of grammatical forms. • Range of grammatical forms used.
Discourse Management *Extent* *Relevance* *Coherence* *Cohesion*	• Stretches of language produced. • Relevance of contributions and organisation of ideas. • Use of appropriate cohesive devices and discourse markers.
Pronunciation *Intonation* *Stress* *Individual sounds*	• Intelligibility • Intonation • Word stress • Individual sounds
Interactive Communication *Initiating* *Responding* *Development*	• Initiating, responding and linking contributions to other speakers' interventions. • Maintaining and developing interaction, and negotiating towards an outcome.

Model answers

Test 1

Model answers – Test 1

The B2 First is usually taken by candidates who want to obtain a B2-level certificate, which corresponds to an upper-intermediate level of English.

As described by the Common European Framework of Reference for Languages (CEFRL), candidates with a B2 level are considered *independent vantage users*, thus being able to:

- understand the main ideas of complex tests

- interact with a certain degree of fluency and spontaneity both in written and oral form

- produce clear and detailed texts on a range of subjects.

The purpose of the following model answers is to provide teachers and candidates with an example of language production and test performance that would score a high mark in a real B2 First Speaking test.

Without being particularly complex, these answers contain grammatical and lexical features as well as a range of discourse resources suited to an upper-intermediate level of English (B2).

Please note that complete linguistic accuracy is not expected at B2 level, but only candidates whose performance is generally accurate will receive a high mark.

On pages 95–100, there are comments highlighting different aspects of the model answers, such as:

- the strategies candidates make use of to address some of the parts

- the ways in which candidates express their opinions

- how candidates interact with one another, etc.

The aim of these comments is to draw the reader's attention to important details that might help to achieve a successful performance in this part of the B2 First examination.

While reading the model answers and the examiner's comments, please bear in mind the following:

- The test is taken in pairs, and candidates are expected to interact with each other.

- The approximate timing of each part of the test is as follows:

    o Part 1: 2 minutes (pair) / 3 minutes (trio)

    o Part 2: 4 minutes (pair) / 6 minutes (trio)

    o Part 3: 4 minutes (pair) / 5 minutes (trio)

    o Part 4: 4 minutes (pair) / 6 minutes (trio)

These model answers would achieve a high score in a B2 First Speaking test, and so should be regarded as strong-performance answers that provide examples of the types of linguistic structures candidates are expected to produce at this level rather than examples of minimum performance to pass.

Test 1 – Part 1 – Model answers

Interlocutor	Where are you from, Candidate A?
Candidate A	*I'm from Costa Rica, and I live in a town called Nicoya.*
Interlocutor	And you, Candidate B?
Candidate B	*I'm from Stockholm in Sweden, but I live in Rome.*
Interlocutor	Are you working or studying at the moment?
Candidate B	*I work for a logistics company as a customer services manager. I've been doing that for about five years.*
Interlocutor	And you?
Candidate A	*Well, I'm working as a sales assistant in a shop, you know, as a temporary job over the summer. But I'm planning to start a college course soon. I want to study computer science.*

Sport

- **When was the last time you played a sport?** *It was probably about a month ago, when I played football with some friends.*
- **Do you prefer individual sport or team sports?** *Well, I'm really into running and I like doing that on my own because I can listen to music.*
- **How often do you watch live sport?** *Well, I watch a lot of football on TV and they show a lot of important matches live. In terms of going to watch matches in person, I tend to watch my local team probably about once a month. It's really good fun even though we usually lose.*
- **Is there a sports event you would really like to go to in the future?** *If I had the chance to go and see some Olympic events, I'm sure it would be an amazing experience to get to see the most famous athletes in the world. But I don't think it's likely because it's so hard to get tickets for those kinds of events.*

Food

- **Do you prefer eating at home or in restaurants?** *I like both, to be honest. Now and then, it's fun to go to a restaurant, especially if you can try some new dishes and enjoy the atmosphere. But deep down, I guess it's more relaxing to have a home-cooked meal with friends.*
- **Tell us about a special meal you can remember.** *Probably when I was invited to the home of an Indian colleague and her family cooked me some incredible traditional dishes. I'd been to Indian restaurants before so I thought I knew what to expect but this was completely different. It was real, authentic Indian food.*
- **Have you ever taken cooking classes?** *Only in school, where the teacher would show us the basics of food preparation. In general, the recipes we got to try were pretty easy. I'd love to learn more about French food, though.*
- **Is there a type of food you'd like to try?** *Well, I'm curious about Vietnamese food. I'm a big fan of Asian cuisine, in other words, anything spicy or with noodles or rice, and as far as know, Vietnamese food is similar. I've also heard that it's quite diverse and healthy too.*

Speaking First

Films

- **Do you prefer watching films at home or going to the cinema?** *Definitely watching films at home. Going to the cinema just costs too much, because you've got to think about transport, tickets, not to mention the snacks as well. I don't see the point when you can just stream one instead.*
- **What type of films do you like the most?** *To be honest, I'm not a huge film fan. I suppose I'd say action films like Mission Impossible because you can just switch your brain off for a while because you don't have to worry about a complicated plot, or whatever. That's the main thing.*
- **Do you have a favourite film from Sweden?** *Well, pretty much everyone has heard of Ingmar Berman's films, I'd imagine. He's a very famous director, and I'd definitely recommend The Seventh Seal. I won't go into the plot because it's quite complex, but some of the scenes are iconic, especially the chess one, so it's worth watching for that reason.*
- **Have you ever wanted to act or make films?** *Well, I used to perform in school plays when I was younger but not anything serious. The idea of making films kind of appeals, though. My friends and I create short videos and upload them to social media. I enjoy the creative aspect of the editing and music, all that stuff.*

Test 1 – Part 2 – Model answers

Being active

Task 1 – Long turn

Interlocutor In this part of the test, I'm going to give each of you two photographs. I'd like you to talk about your photographs on your own for about a minute, and also to answer a question about your partner's photographs. *(Candidate A)* It's your turn first. Here are your photographs (photo A – three young people looking at a laptop and taking notes, photo B – children listening to a teacher in a classroom). They show people studying in different ways. I'd like you to compare the photographs, and say what you think the people in these photos are enjoying about studying in these ways. All right?

Candidate A *OK, well, in the first picture there are three students who appear to be in a computer lab or somewhere like that. They may be working on a project together because the student with glasses looks like he's going to take notes. By contrast, the second picture is what I'd call a traditional classroom, with pupils sitting at separate desks, and the teacher explaining the information. One of the students has raised his hand so he might have misunderstood something.*

Obviously, these photos illustrate two rather different approaches to studying or education. The students in the first picture are finding information for themselves, whereas in the classroom, the students' role is more passive. What I mean is that they're simply listening. Also, the students in the classroom look younger, so they're probably at school, whereas I'd guess the others are college or university students. Turning to what they might be enjoying about studying, well, the college students look very engaged, probably because they're giving their input and making decisions for themselves. With the second photo, the students can receive instant help by asking questions, and that can be motivating. I think this shows us the importance of getting feedback or support.

Interlocutor Thank you. (Candidate B), do you often use the internet for your studies?

Candidate B	*Well, in terms of language learning, I do, yes. You can find all sorts of useful videos to practise listening and I try to read online articles on a daily basis. And of course, the vast majority of information on social media is in English too, so that's another useful way to improve your skills.*
Interlocutor	Thank you. (*Can I have the booklet, please?*) Now, (*Candidate B*), here are your photographs. They show people shopping for clothes in different ways (photo A – a man using a computer to look at a clothing website, photo B – two women in a clothes shop, about to try on items). I'd like you to compare **two** of the photographs, and say why you think the people have chosen to shop for clothes in these ways. All right?
Candidate B	*Yes, OK, let's see. I'll start with the photo of the man. He seems to be at home, using a laptop to do some online shopping. It looks as if it's the website of a footwear company. He appears to be looking at men's shoes, so he might be choosing shoes for himself. In the photo, the man seems to be ready to pay for the item so he has probably made his decision. And of course, it's much more convenient to do that online instead of going around all the shops in person.*
	As for the second picture, I'd guess that those shoppers are more likely to make a purchase. We can see two young women in a fitting room of a shop. In particular, the one on the right has selected various items of clothing which she's about to try on. There's more of a sense of excitement about shopping in this photo, so I get the impression that they wanted to have a fun day out together rather than the convenience of online shopping.
Interlocutor	Thank you. (*Candidate A*), do you prefer shopping for clothes with other people or alone?
Candidate A	*Well, it depends. Things like t-shirts, well, I already have an idea of how they're going to fit and what suits me so it's pretty easy just to shop by myself. But if I do need a second opinion, I prefer going with my sister or a friend. Actually, my sister helped me pick an outfit for our cousin's wedding.*
Interlocutor	Thank you. (*Can I have the booklet, please?*)

Test 1 – Part 3 – Model answers

Attracting young professionals

Collaborative task

Interlocutor	Now, I'd like you to talk about something together for about **two** minutes. I'd like you to imagine that a city is preparing an advertising campaign to attract more young professionals to live in the area. Here are some ideas they are thinking about and a question for you to discuss. First you have some time to look at the task. Now, talk to each other about why these factors would make young professionals want to live in the city.
Candidate A	*Well then, would you like to start?*
Candidate B	*Sure, let's see. Well, obviously if you were thinking of moving to a new area, you'd want to know whether it's safe, so you'd probably research the crime rates, wouldn't you? But if we're talking specifically about young professionals, they'd probably have accommodation at the top of their list. What do you think?*
Candidate A	*Yes, that's right. I don't know about you, but I sort of imagine people at the start of their careers, so a city with a range of affordable places to rent would be ideal. And if they can find attractive accommodation near where they work, it'll presumably save them time in terms of*

Speaking First

	commuting. But I suppose that brings us to transport. Do you think that would be an important consideration?
Candidate B	*Oh, most definitely, it's one they should think about if they've got family in other parts of the country. And they might be asked to travel a lot for work as well. They're more important than cinemas or restaurants, for example, although you might disagree.*
Candidate A	*Well, I see your point and I do think transport is vital, but you seem to put it ahead of leisure facilities. For me, they're probably of equal importance because moving to a new city is a major decision, isn't it? Would you really be willing to move somewhere if there was nothing to do, or no ways of making new friends?*
Candidate B	*That's true. So if we look at it as a permanent move, then you might also look at other things too, like schools and hospitals. You'd want to settle somewhere that has facilities for children, for example.*
Candidate A	*Yes, I hadn't thought about that but it makes sense. In fact, I'd argue they're all important..*
Interlocutor	Thank you. Now you have about a minute to decide which idea would be the best for the town.
Candidate B	*Perhaps you'd like to start this time?*
Candidate A	*Of course, it seems that we both feel that young professionals are likely to pay particular attention to transport and accommodation, don't we? If so, the city should probably focus on those in their advertising campaigns. Do you agree?*
Candidate B	*Well, I suppose so. I mean, obviously the city should highlight all the other factors too, especially if they are strengths.*
Candidate A	*Mmm.. so are you saying that the city should analyse what it does best and build their advertising around that? I'm not sure about that. It would be better to put transport and accommodation at the centre of the advertising. Accommodation will definitely attract young professionals because it's so hard to find places to live.*
Candidate B	*Don't get me wrong, we're on the same page. The city should focus on accommodation to attract young professionals, and maybe this could be linked to information about efficient transport connections too. But as well as that, it should mention other aspects so as to boost their chances of success.*
Candidate A	*Great, so I think we're in agreement then.*

Test 1 – Part 4 – Model answers

Question-based discussion

Interlocutor	As well as young professionals, what other types of people might cities want to attract?
Candidate A	*Well, honestly, there needs to be as much diversity as possible. What I mean is that cities rely on all sorts of residents, including families, students, retired people or whatever. You see, they all have a role to play in society because they have different skills and experiences, don't they? I'd argue that this mix of perspectives builds strong communities.*
Interlocutor	Some people believe that it is unfair for cities to receive so much investment and that rural areas should be improved instead. Do you agree?
Candidate B	*Well, as we've been discussing, I don't see it that way at all. The truth is that investing in cities makes the most sense because it'll have the biggest impact on more people. For example,*

	there are so many people commuting to cities each day for work, so it makes sense that the public transport links are upgraded there first. But it's still important to invest in rural areas too.
Interlocutor	*(Candidate A),* what do you think?
Candidate A	*I'm not sure really. I guess these sorts of decisions have to be taken after weighing up many important factors. In my country, for instance, a lot of investment has gone into improving living standards in rural areas, and to a certain extent it has sort of encouraged more young people to settle in those places instead of migrating to cities.*
Interlocutor	What can companies do to help staff who have just moved to the area?
Candidate A	*That's a difficult question. If you mean the things that we've already been talking about, they could offer free transport passes or help employees find somewhere to live. And I've heard that some companies even provide accommodation for staff, which would be very useful.*
Interlocutor	*(Candidate B),* do you agree?
Candidate B	*Well, they're definitely good suggestions but I'd like to add something. What about organising social activities? It doesn't have to be anything fancy, but maybe a night out at a restaurant with colleagues? It would help break the ice which in turn would make the new employees feel more settled.*
Interlocutor	What are the most enjoyable things to do on a city break in Nicoya?
Candidate A	*Well, if you're talking about a couple of days, I'd personally say walking up La Cruz hill is a must because you'll get an amazing panoramic view of the whole town. To make the most of it, you should aim to go there at sunset. Oh, and I'd recommend checking out the farmers' market where you can try so many delicious local specialities. You won't regret it, trust me!*
Interlocutor	Some people say that remote working will transform cities. What do you think?
Candidate B	*Do you mean in terms of what people use cities for? As far as the numbers of people in city centres are concerned, the impact can already be seen because some city centres are far quieter than they once were. On the face of it, that sounds like a positive. After all, less traffic congestion will eventually benefit the environment. But what about local businesses? I say this with a heavy heart because many of the places where I loved killing time with friends are closing down. So given all that, I'd basically say it's true, but I hope they don't turn into ghost towns.*
Interlocutor	Would you agree that cities are designed for the needs of young people?
Candidate A	*I don't know if I can answer objectively, but I suppose they are, to be honest. Cities are vibrant, fast-paced places that are always changing, and I associate that more with young people. On top of that, most cities have entertainment venues, universities and places like that right in the heart of things. It makes sense, because young people are the ones who tend to drive less so they need to have easy access to those sorts of amenities.*
Interlocutor	Thank you. That is the end of the test.

Examiner comments

Test 1

Speaking First

Examiner comments

Test 1 – Part 1 – Model answers

In Part 1, candidates are asked about themselves, their backgrounds and experiences. These questions are scripted, and the interlocutor will never improvise them. Candidates are expected to answer and justify their responses, but these should not turn into a long monologue. If the answer given to a question is particularly short, the examiner will probably ask a follow-up question such as "Why?" or "Why not?". Therefore, candidates should answer more than a simple "Yes", "No" or one-word answer, but not much more.

For example:

Question	Are you working or studying at the moment?
Answer	I work for a logistics company as a customer services manager. I've been doing that for about five years.

Given the nature of the conversation, these answers should sound natural and non-rehearsed. Sounding natural is part of being fluent in a language, so using some informal expressions (e.g. *all that stuff*), contractions (e.g. *I've, that's not*) or discourse markers *(e.g. well, in other words*) is actually encouraged, as long as the language sounds natural and is not used excessively. Examiners may politely interrupt candidates if they are giving lengthy responses in Part 1 that sound unnatural or rehearsed.

As this is a B2-level speaking test, candidates' answers should show B2-level grammar and vocabulary, even in Part 1, if possible. For this reason, in the model answers provided for Part 1, there are some appropriate B2-level phrases like:

- *In terms of*
- *tend to*
- *get to see*
- *now and then*
- *deep down*

- *in general*
- *in other words*
- *not to mention*
- *I won't go into*
- *etc.*

Part 1 is probably not the most suitable part for candidates to prove their level, but they should still try to show what they know, and, above all, try to sound natural.

Key things to practise:

- Talking about personal background referring to past, present and future situations
- Providing brief examples to illustrate points (e.g. *for instance…like Mission Impossible*)
- Using phrases to express likes, interests or preferences (e.g. *…I'm really into running, I'd definitely recommend…I'd love to learn, I'm a big fan of…*)

Test 1 – Part 2 – Model answers

As with Part 1, the focus of Part 2 is individual speaking. In an individual long turn of one minute without interruption, each candidate is asked to compare two pictures and answer a question about them. They will also have to answer a follow-up question regarding their partner's pictures.

This is a chance for candidates to show how well they can speak on their own in a longer turn. Candidates' grammar and vocabulary are expected to be excellent and, more specifically in this part, there is special emphasis on their discourse management – i.e. how long they can speak for (*extent*), how relevant their contributions (*relevance*) are, and how well they can organise and connect their speech (*coherence* and *cohesion*).

Please note that it is common for candidates to be interrupted when the time is up before they have finished. However, this does not mean that it will affect the candidate's mark negatively, as long as what he/she has said has been delivered using B2-level grammar and vocabulary in a well-organised speech.

Notice the following elements in the sample answers on pages 89–93:

The language candidates use

If we take a look at Candidate A's and Candidate B's turns, we notice that they:

- **use appropriate B2 grammar and lexis:** *who appear to be…with what I'd call…with pupils sitting at separate desks…the students' role is more passive…the students look very engaged…they're giving their input…the importance of getting feedback…browsing rather than paying for the item…likely to make a purchase…a sense of excitement…the convenience of online shopping…etc.*

- **use cohesive devices and discourse markers to organise his/her speech:** *By contrast… Turning to…with the second photo…I'll start with the…As for the second photo…In particular…whereas…also…etc.*

- **goes beyond description by speculating:** *They may be working on…looks like he's going to…might have misunderstood something…they're probably at school…I think this shows…it looks as if…he could be just seeing…I'd guess that…I get the impression that…etc.*

These expressions show that candidates are capable of comparing, speculating about and offering opinions on visual stimuli and broader themes.

How candidates organise their speech

It's also important to notice how both candidates organise their speech as they use different strategies to approach this part of the test.

Candidate A chooses to briefly describe both pictures first. Then he/she compares them, pointing out the main differences and, finally, he/she addresses the question directly (*What are the people enjoying about studying in these ways?*).

By contrast, Candidate B focuses on each picture separately, describing each picture in more detail, comparing the second picture with the first and providing an answer to the question (*Why have the people chosen to shop for clothes in these ways?*) for each picture in turn.

Both of these approaches to the task are valid, but it's important to note that candidates should include some comparison and speculation in their long turns, rather than simply describing their pictures. They have up to 60 seconds to provide their answers.

Follow-up question

After the individual turn, the interlocutor will ask the other candidate a question related to the topic their partner has just been discussing.

Sometimes, the question will require the candidate to refer directly to the pictures (e.g. *Which one do you prefer?*), or it might be a more general question related to the topic (e.g. *How often do you buy clothes online?*). The candidate should answer this question in about thirty seconds.

Key things to practise:

- Making the connection between an image and the general question (e.g. *I think this shows us the importance of getting feedback or support…*)
- Speculating (e.g. *The people may be working on a project together…might have misunderstood something…he might be choosing a gift…*)
- Justifying ideas (e.g. *…because the student with glasses looks like he's going to take notes.*)

Test 1 – Part 3 – Model answers

Part 3 is the main collaborative task of the exam, meaning that the interaction will be between the candidates rather than the candidate and examiner. Candidates will hold a conversation about a conversation that is presented in the form of a question and some prompts that provide ideas for this conversation.

The main focus of this part of the test is interactive communication, so there is special emphasis on assessing skills such as giving and asking for opinions, justifying their answers, agreeing and disagreeing, making decisions and so on. Candidates need to demonstrate turn-taking skills and the ability to respond to each other.

Notice the following elements in the model answers:

The language candidates use

Throughout the Part 3 model answers, we notice that both candidates:

- **use appropriate B2 grammar and lexis:** *research the crime rates…talking specifically about… a range of affordable accommodation…presumably…in terms of commuting…consideration… it's one they should think about…put it ahead of…look at it as a permanent move… settle somewhere…would you be willing to …if there was…?…pay particular attention to… this could be linked to…so as to boost their chances of success…etc.*

- **ask for and give opinions:** *What do you think?…I don't know about you, but I sort of imagine…I suppose…Do you think that…?…For me…I do think…I'd argue…Perhaps you'd like to start this time?…would you like to start?…wouldn't you?…although you might disagree…so are you saying that…?…Do you agree?…etc.*

- **agree and disagree:** *Yes, that's right …Oh, most definitely…I see your point…That's true…It seems we both feel that…I hadn't though about that…I'm not sure about that…I suppose so…Don't get me wrong…we're on the same page…we're in agreement…etc.*

These expressions show that candidates are capable of initiating, responding and linking contributions to each other's turn, and that they can develop a successful interaction and negotiate towards an outcome in a very natural way.

In this case, both candidates reach an agreement by the end. However, this is by no means a test requirement and candidates' marks will not be affected by whether an agreement or conclusion is reached or not.

Finally, it is extremely important that this part does not turn into two separate, individual turns at speaking rather than a seamless interaction. Therefore, candidates should avoid lengthy answers and should try to involve their partner at the end of each turn to keep the conversation flowing.

Key things to practise:

- Building on the partner's turn by referring to their ideas (e.g. *I suppose that brings us to…you seem to put it ahead of…it seems that we both feel…etc.*)

Test 1 – Part 4 – Model answers

Part 4 builds on the discussion topic explored in Part 3. The examiner asks a series of discussion questions which the candidates are expected to develop using a range of communicative and interactive strategies (such as those demonstrated in Part 3). The questions are usually more complex and require students to move away from personal experiences to discuss subjects in a broader way. Candidates should attempt to give insightful and well-organised answers and include a good range of B2 grammar and vocabulary.

The examiner may invite one of the candidates to comment on what their partner has said (e.g. *do you agree?*).

As with previous parts of the test, candidates are advised to show that they are paying attention to what their partner is saying. This will enable them to link ideas well.

Candidates' interaction

Some examples of strong answers are the following:

Interlocutor	*As well as young professionals, what other types of people might cities want to attract?*
Candidate	*Well, honestly, there needs to be as much diversity as possible. What I mean is that cities rely on all sorts of residents, including families, students, retired people or whatever. You see, they all have a role to play in society because they have different skills and experiences, don't they? I'd argue that this mix of perspectives builds strong communities.*

In the answer above, the candidate uses an appropriate discourse marker (*What I mean is that…*) to expand on their initial idea (*there needs to be as much diversity as possible*) with justification (*…they all have a role to play in society*). We also note the use of appropriate B2 language and natural conversational fillers and vague expressions (*or whatever, you see*)

The following example also shows some great interaction in Part 3:

Interlocutor	*Some people believe that it is unfair for cities to receive so much investment and that rural areas should be improved instead. Do you agree?*
Candidate	*Well, as we've been discussing, I don't see it that way at all. The truth is that investing in cities makes the most sense because it'll have the biggest impact on more people. For example, there are so many people commuting to cities each day for work, so it makes sense that the public transport links are upgraded there first. But it's still important to invest in rural areas too.*

Here, the candidate is clearly and strongly disagreeing with the statement provided by the examiner (*I don't see it that way at all*) and he/she then justifies it with a clear reason (*The truth is that investing in cities makes the most sense because it will have the biggest impact on more people.*) and then develops this further with an example (*For example, there are so many people commuting to cities each day for work, so it makes sense that the public transports are upgraded there first…*).

It is worth emphasising that at the strong B2 level, candidates are expected to use a range of linguistic features, as shown in the following answer:

Speaking First

Interlocutor	*Some people say that remote working will transform cities. What do you think?*
Candidate	*Do you mean in terms of what people use cities for? As far as the numbers of people in city centres are concerned, the impact can already be seen because some city centres are far quieter than they once were. On the face of it, that sounds like a positive. After all, less traffic congestion will eventually benefit the environment. But what about local businesses? I say this with a heavy heart because many of the places where I loved killing time with friends are closing down. So given all that, I'd basically say it's true, but I hope they don't turn into ghost towns.*

Note the use of idiomatic language, clear attempts to organise information, modal and passive constructions, speculation and a natural 'round-off' phrase to signal that their turn is about to end (*So given all that, I'd basically say...*).

Key things to practise:

- Framing a subject or question (e.g. *If you're talking about…Do you mean in terms of…?...As far as…is concerned…etc.)*

Throughout the model answers provided by candidates in every part of Test 1, we can see that they:

- use B2-level structures
- sound very natural
- are well connected and organised
- attempt to keep the discussion going by referring back to their partner.

www.ingramcontent.com/pod-product-compliance
Lightning Source LLC
Chambersburg PA
CBHW081918090526
44590CB00019B/3405